SKI TOWN
Après Ski

APPETIZING PLATES *and* HANDCRAFTED COCKTAILS
from WORLD CLASS SKI RESORTS

JENNIE IVERSON

SECOND EDITION

23 22 21 20 19   7 6 5 4 3

Library of Congress: 2014913554

ISBN 13: 978-0-9857290-4-2

Manufactured in China by Pettit Network Inc.

For photography credits, see end section.
Book Design and typesetting by James Monroe Design, LLC.

For information about special purchases or custom editions, please contact: info@skitownlife.com. Ski Town Group, Ltd. is the publishing firm for Ski Town Life.

Ski Town Life
2121 N. Frontage Road, W. #5
Vail, Colorado 81657

www.skitownlife.com

 @skitownlife

 @skitownlife

 skitownlife

Ski Town Après Ski *is dedicated to Ross and our family of boys—Hunter, Grant and Brooks.*

My little masters, pour yourselves Kiddie Cocktails and raise your glasses in a toast:
Cheers to a blue bird day on the mountain, followed by gourmet snacks
in front of a roaring fire.

CONTENTS

CONTENTS
Listed by Ski Resort

FOREWORD

When I traded in my small ski hill in the suburbs of Minneapolis for the intimidating Rocky Mountains, I was 12 years old. I had little confidence in my downhill skiing. Ski Club Vail approached me as if they knew—in years to come—I would receive my Olympic gold medal. The program allowed me to become familiar with Vail's community: a collective unit that works together, a ski town that has heart and pride in what they do. Ski Club Vail, and my success, is a result of this strong, passionate community involvement.

Two knee surgeries later, I've had the time to reflect back on what made me love skiing, what gave me the drive to keep going, and why, after everything, it remains an important part of me. It's because skiing is a tradition. My dad devoted much of his life to skiing, as my grandfather had. They introduced me to the snow and their passion became mine. For me, the mountains are a place of solidarity where I can focus on myself. After that individual time, après ski is an important part of my day; it's a time to relax, warm up, and reflect on the day's events with others.

Pepi's Restaurant & Bar is my family's after-skiing tradition. Pepi Gramshammer, a ski legend, and his wife Sheika brought Austria to Vail, Colorado with their gasthof (European-style inn) that is still thriving since it's opening in 1964. Their love for Vail, the mountains, and keeping Vail the way it was back in the 1960s is why I always come back. It's nice to know that there will always be Pepi's at the bottom of the mountain at the end of a long day.

Now acclimated to Europe and their traditions, the meaning of après ski has changed for me—mostly in the foods and drinks. In Austria, Germany, and Switzerland, I found that the best way to practice my German was with a warm glass of glühwein—red wine stewed with citrus and sweet spices. As if that's not the perfect cap to a long ski day, the Europeans also have two very delicious and very deadly desserts: kaiserschmarrn and germknödel. The first is a blend between a light French toast and a pancake topped with raisins and powdered sugar. The second is a yeast dumpling with a special plum filling and topped with poppy seeds, sugar and butter. Good thing après ski is about sharing!

No matter what part of the world I'm in, or what I'm eating or drinking, I always find the meaning of skiing in the après ski scene. Skiing isn't just a sport, Vail isn't just a ski town, and après is not just a prefix. The time we give to each other and the things we love are what make us who we are.

With many thanks to those who have come before me, to those who have helped me and to all those young skiers after me.

Warm wishes,

Lindsey Vonn

Ski Town Après Ski Background

The *Ski Town Après Ski* cookbook showcases a blended passion for unique appetizers, handcrafted cocktails, skiing and traveling. This is a must-have souvenir for skiers, foodies, libation-lovers and travelers. Like *Ski Town Soups* (the first cookbook in the Ski Town Group offering), *Ski Town Après Ski* is a beautiful, colorful rendition of over 60 North American world-class ski resorts, fun-loving restaurants, gourmet appetizers and revitalizing cocktails. Take note of the various eclectic flavor profiles with regional flair; many of the inspired recipes originate from fresh and locally-sourced ingredients, which are close to the chefs' hearts and elevate the ski town cuisine. If you have spent time in a mountain village, you understand the celebration that occurs around the Après Ski culture. This is a time after the mountain closes when friends and family share stories of their ski day, enjoy live music and generally socialize (while oftentimes wearing ski gear). Pull up a slope side beach chair on the snow and indulge in this cookbook for a taste and visual tour of the après scene. This cookbook is a toast to culinary delights, which will help you celebrate as you gather with family and friends for après ski after a perfect day on the mountain. Let the après-atmosphere envelop you!

Winning Restaurants Determined

To determine the included restaurants, Ski Town Group, Ltd. conducted extensive online research, along with periodical ratings and guidance. The après scene was incredibly important when it came to choosing the featured restaurants. The unique food offerings and extensive libations as well as the restaurants' culture and ambiance all factored into the selection process. Restaurant reviews and recommendations, both online and through travelers/guests, were taken into account. Based on the research results, the *Ski Town Après Ski* cookbook highlights chef-chosen appetizer and small plate recipes, along with bartender or mixologist-chosen cocktails, from the most beloved après ski restaurants in over 60 world-class North American ski towns. The restaurants range from high-end, fine dining locations to bars and pubs. The restaurants are located in the same ski town as the ski resort, or relatively close to the associated ski resort.

Cookbook Usability

This cookbook is divided into 5 sections: Bites & Nibbles, Sea & Surf, Land & Turf, Sweet Treats and Handcrafted Cocktails. Two Tables of Contents: 1 – by food or drink category and 2 – by ski resort. This usability appeals to foodies, home cooks, aspiring drink-makers, as well as travelers and skiers. Finally, there is nothing more tempting than a well-constructed appetizer paired perfectly with a luscious cocktail. With most food recipes, there is a cocktail suggestion in the Serving Suggestion part of the recipe.

The green circle indicates a relatively easy recipe, to be tackled late in the day or on a weeknight. The green circle recipes 🟢 should be approachable to all cooks. The blue square 🟦 is a bit more difficult, but within most home cooks' capabilities. The black diamond ◆ recipes are the most advanced recipes in the cookbook, and may challenge even the most adept home cook. Sample black diamond recipes when ample time is available. Have fun with these ratings! It's not a scientific rating system; levels of difficulty were merely estimated by amount of time to complete the recipe and number and availability of the ingredients.

Own the Collection

The Ski Town Cookbook Collection is comprised of over 400 recipes from unique venues across North American ski towns.

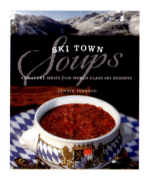

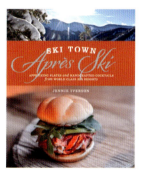

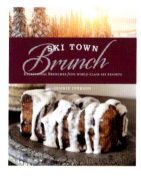

Ski Town Soups presents a perfectly balanced recipe for life: a ski town, a comfortable restaurant, and a yummy bowl of soup.

Ski Town Après Ski captures the essence of the après ski scene by pairing appetizing plates and handcrafted cocktails.

Ski Town Brunch highlights recipes from charming bed and breakfasts to luxury resorts, setting an energizing tone for the rest of the day.

Ski Town Journey Continued

Purchase the box set or individual titles through our retail partners or at **SkiTownLife.com**. Sign-up at **SkiTownLife.com** for custom recipes to add to your collection, newsletter and blog posts, and other interesting culinary tidbits.

BITES & NIBBLES

BITES & NIBBLES
continued

LOCAL BEET CHIPS
with Curried Yogurt

GOURMANDIE • CHEF EMILY LEVINE • SANDPOINT, IDAHO

After participating in a year-long local food challenge in Northern Minnesota, Chef Emily's passion for local food continues to grow in the form of Red Wheelbarrow Produce, a small farm in the valley north of Sandpoint that Emily owns and operates. Being the chef at Gourmandie balances her 9-month farming habit, helps hone her culinary skills and inspires dishes like this one—using stored beets with immense color and nutrient-dense flesh to make a stunning display with extreme flavor.

1 lb. baseball-sized local beets
(a mix of red and golden varieties)

1 Tbsp. olive oil

½ tsp. salt

Curried Yogurt

S ERVES **4**

Preheat oven to 350 degrees. Peel beets and slice with a mandolin. Toss in a bowl with olive oil, making sure to coat all surfaces. Spread beets evenly on a baking sheet and sprinkle with salt. Place a second baking sheet on top of the beets and bake for 10 minutes. Remove top baking sheet and continue baking uncovered until the beets are dry to the center. Beets on the outer edges of the baking sheets may dry-out earlier, so remove finished beets when ready, returning the rest to finish baking. The beets will not feel crispy until they have cooled completely.

CURRIED YOGURT

½ cup whole milk plain yogurt

½ tsp. curry powder

½ tsp. salt

Water or milk to thin

Mix all ingredients together, adding water to thin to a dip consistency. The beet chips are relatively fragile so err on the side of a thinner dip.

SERVING SUGGESTION:

Serve beet chips with Curried Yogurt alongside a nice red table wine, like the offering from Small House Winery, which sources its grapes from Idaho, Washington and Oregon, and where all wine is produced in Sandpoint, Idaho.

BAKED LILLE
with Maple Pumpkin Butter

OKEMO MOUNTAIN RESORT • CHEF SCOT EMERSON • LUDLOW, VERMONT

Vermont is world-renowned for its food products, commitment to the food culture and food sustainability. Last year, Vermont Farmstead and five other Vermont cheese makers won international recognition with their blue ribbon winning cheeses. Vermont Farmstead Lille was one of those cheeses. As Vermont Farmstead's chef partner, Scot Emerson created his Baked Lille with Maple Pumpkin Butter in a video series for the Vermont Department of Agriculture.

7 oz. Vermont Farmstead Lille cheese

2 oz. Fox Meadow Maple Pumpkin Butter

3 sheets phyllo dough

2 oz. Cabot Butter

2 graham crackers, crushed

SERVES 4

Over low heat, melt butter. Lay out 1 phyllo sheet and gently brush with butter. Lay a second sheet on the first and gently brush this with butter. On phyllo, sprinkle crushed graham crackers, and then top with the third phyllo sheet and gently brush this with butter. Cut the phyllo in half; you will have 2 rectangles (approximately 8 x 6-inches).

The lille is a cylinder, so cut it in half (you will have 2 cylinders). Place one piece of cheese in the middle of each sheet of phyllo with the cut-side facing up. Place approximately 1 oz. of maple pumpkin butter on each piece of cheese. Make a beggar's purse by folding the corners of the phyllo over the top of the cheese. Bake at 400 degrees for about 10 minutes or until golden brown.

SERVING SUGGESTION:

Enjoy this decadent appetizer with the delicious S'moretini, HANDCRAFTED COCKTAIL section.

BLUE MOOSE PIZZA SLIDERS

BLUE MOOSE PIZZA • CORPORATE CHEF JAY MCCARTHY • AVON, COLORADO

Proudly serving hand-tossed NY Style pizzas in Beaver Creek for over 18 years, Blue Moose is strongly connected to the Colorado roots and they showcase Colorado craft beers at the restaurants. Nothing finishes off a big day on the mountain quite as well as a few Blue Moose Pizza Sliders and a refreshing draft beer brewed locally in the Valley or down in the Front Range. On the menu, Blue Moose also offers an après slider combo, featuring three Blue Moose Pizza Sliders and a sampling of three of Colorado's best brews: Crazy Mountain Brewery's Amber Ale (Edwards, CO), Bonfire Brewery's Firestarter IPA (Eagle, CO) and New Belgium Brewing's Fat Tire Amber Ale (Fort Collins, CO).

3 cups all purpose flour

1 package Fleischmann's Rapid Rise Yeast

1 ½ tsp. salt

3 tsp. sugar

1 cup warm water

2 Tbsp. olive or vegetable oil

Basil, chopped

Blue Moose Sauce

2 cups mozzarella cheese, shredded

4 oz. pepperoni or salami, thinly sliced

S ERVES DESIRED PARTY SIZE

To create the Blue Moose hand-made dough, place yeast, warm water, sugar and basil in a mixer with a dough hook; mix for 2 minutes at low speed. Add salt and oil, then mix for 90 seconds at slow speed. Add flour, then mix for 9 minutes at slow speed. Remove dough from mixer and cut into desired portions. Cover and refrigerate for at least 15 minutes, or up to 48 hours.

Divide dough in half. Divide one half into 1-oz. portions. Roll each portion out into a thin 3-inch disk. Shape edge into standing rim of dough. Spread Blue Moose Sauce, cheese and pepperoni or salami on pizzas, dividing evenly. Bake pizzas at 450 degrees for 15 minutes or until cheese is melted and lightly browned. Cut into wedges.

BLUE MOOSE SAUCE

10 oz. tomato puree

1 Tbsp. oregano, dried

½ Tbsp. basil, dried

½ Tbsp. salt

2 oz. olive oil

1 Tbsp. garlic, diced

¼ Tbsp. black pepper

1 Tbsp. sugar

1 tsp. ground fennel

¼ cup red wine

10—12 cups water to consistency

In a bowl, combine pizza sauce ingredients. Reserve.

SERVING SUGGESTION:
Pair these with a Colorado craft beer!

CABOT CHEDDAR FONDUE

MAD RIVER GLEN • CHEF MICHAEL WITZEL • WAITSFIELD, VERMONT

Mad River Glen chef Michael Witzel and Cabot Creamery host a Free Fondue Après party throughout the ski season. This recipe can be sampled there or in the intimacy of your own kitchen (cut this recipe in half for a family like gathering).

16 oz. dark beer (Wolaver's Oatmeal Stout, recommended)

3 lbs. Cabot Extra Sharp Cheddar, shredded

2 Tbsp. flour

1 Tbsp. red pepper

1 Tbsp. dried mustard

1 Tbsp. dried thyme

1 Tbsp. dried parsley

1 Tbsp. garlic powder

2 Tbsp. onion powder

1 cup sour cream

SERVES 12

EASIEST

Bring beer and spices to a simmer in a heavy saucepan. Add cheese, handfuls at a time, whipping constantly so not to burn. Add flour to bind the oils in the cheese to help from breaking. Finish with sour cream.

SERVING SUGGESTION:

Serve in a crockpot with sliced baguettes and sliced apples for dipping. This recipe goes perfectly with a refreshing mug of beer.

BRUSSEL SPROUTS
with Lemon, Honey, Garlic & Walnuts

TERRA BISTRO • VAIL, COLORADO

At Terra Bistro, nature yields fine dining. Borrowing the Latin word for Earth in its name, Terra Bistro has been transforming whole foods into gourmet innovations for more than 20 years. Earning accolades from such publications as Gourmet Magazine *and the* New York Times, *Terra Bistro is nationally considered a leader in the gourmet green movement.*

2 lbs. brussel sprouts, trimmed and quartered

¼ cup vegetable oil

½ cup walnut pieces, toasted

Sea salt to taste

1 cup honey

½ cup olive oil

1 Tbsp. garlic, minced

2 lemons, zested

S ERVES 6

EASIEST

Preheat oven to 400 degrees. Toss brussel sprouts with vegetable oil and arrange evenly on a cookie sheet. Bake until caramelized and tender. Meanwhile, make the glaze by blending together honey, olive oil, garlic and lemon zest. Mix baked brussel sprouts with toasted walnuts, add glaze to coat and season with sea salt to taste.

SERVING SUGGESTION:
Serve with one of the many cocktails offered by Terra Bistro.

BUFFALO WINGS

THE MATTERHORN • STOWE, VERMONT

Touted as Stowe's world-famous party spot, The Matterhorn offers an expansive menu, as well as thrilling entertainment.

60 jumbo wings

1 gallon canola oil

Wing sauce

SERVES 8

Heat oil to highest temperature and deep-fry wings until interior is fully cooked and skin starts to crisp. Toss the finished wings in the Wing Sauce until they have an even coating. Chill wings in refrigerator. When ready to serve, heat them up at oven's hottest temperature. Toss as needed until all skin turns crispy and golden brown.

WING SAUCE

1 lb. unsalted butter

¼ gallon Louisiana Red Hot sauce

Melt butter and stir in hot sauce.

BLUE CHEESE DRESSING

2 cups sour cream

1 ½ cups mayonnaise

1 Tbsp. Worcestershire sauce

3 dashes Tabasco

½ Tbsp. onion powder

½ Tbsp. granulated garlic

1 cup blue cheese crumbles

Salt and pepper to taste

Mix together all ingredients, except crumbles. When fully mixed, add the crumbles. Add salt and pepper to taste.

SERVING SUGGESTION:
Serve wings with Blue Cheese Dressing on the side. Enjoy this satisfying appetizer with a local beer, like the Switchback from Burlington, Vermont.

STRAWBERRY BRIE BRUSCHETTA

OLD TOWN PUB AND RESTAURANT • STEAMBOAT SPRINGS, COLORADO

Old Town Pub and Restaurant is legendary, featuring an all-from-scratch menu and creatively delicious specialty drinks. The "Pub" is a historic landmark bringing familiar classics to a whole new level, much like the traditional mozzarella bruschetta with this refreshing twist - Strawberry Brie Bruschetta.

3 strawberries, sliced

4 slices Brie cheese

1 loaf French bread, ½-inch slices

1 tsp. sugar

4 basil leaves, chiffonade (cut into long, thin strips)

1 cup balsamic vinegar

¼ cup honey

SERVES 1 - 2

EASIEST

Combine balsamic vinegar with honey, put on high heat and let reduce until it is down to $\frac{1}{3}$ cup. Take off heat and let cool.

Cut strawberries and toss in sugar. Set aside. Top 4 slices of bread with 4 slices of Brie; melt in oven on broil. When cheese is melted and sides of bread are golden brown, pull out of oven and lay strawberries evenly over the four slices. Drizzle balsamic reduction over the top and on the plate, then top bruschetta with basil strips.

SERVING SUGGESTION:
Enjoy with a Spring into the Rockies Martini,
HANDCRAFTED COCKTAIL section.

ASPEN MOUNTAIN

CHEESY PULL APART BREAD

J-BAR AT HOTEL JEROME • CHEF ROB ZACK • ASPEN, COLORADO

Exciting culinary concepts resound in Hotel Jerome, as it is Chef Rob Zack's mission to create an elevated yet approachable dining experience with regionally inspired dishes that delight. Chef Rob, an ultra-popular Aspen chef, delivers and positions Hotel Jerome as a local dining landmark.

1 lb. spicy Italian sausage

2 Tbsp. garlic, minced

1 tsp. chili flakes

1 cup caramelized onions

2 tsp. fennel seed

1 cup provolone cheese, grated

1 cup ricotta cheese

1 cup mascarpone cheese

1 cup parmesan cheese, grated

¼ cup butter, softened

2 sour dough loaves, unsliced

Serves 8 - 10

Sauté sausage over medium heat until cooked through. Add garlic, chili flakes, caramelized onions and fennel seed. Cook for 5 minutes. Remove and place in a mixing bowl with all the rendered fat. Reserve ¼ cup of each cheese then stir remaining ingredients into sausage mixture to combine well. Cut each loaf into a 1-inch checkerboard pattern, being careful not to cut all the way through the loaf. Stuff the filling into each cut. Bake each loaf in a 325-degree oven until the bread is crisp and the filling is hot and bubbly, approximately 15 minutes. Top with the reserved cheese and bake an additional 5 minutes or until the cheese is melted.

SERVING SUGGESTION:
Serve the bread with warm marinara sauce and accompany with The Frontier cocktail, HANDCRAFTED COCKTAIL section.

SMOKED TROUT DEVILED EGGS

DALY'S PUB AT MONTAGE DEER VALLEY • PARK CITY, UTAH

If you think deviled eggs are only for picnics and family reunion buffets, think again. Paired with a frosty glass of Montage Mountain Ale, the Smoked Trout Deviled Eggs at Daly's Pub—served with spicy pickles, fire-roasted flat bread and crispy Edwards ham—are comfort food for foodies.

12 large eggs

1 piping bag of Deviled Egg Filling

Piment D'Espelette to taste (a type of pepper)

SERVES 8

Hard boil eggs in a pot of boiling water by simmering for 12 minutes. Allow eggs time to cool under running water. Peel and chill until thoroughly cold. Cut in half from end to end and remove the yolk. Reserve the 24 white halves for presentation and reserve the yolks for the filling.

To assemble Smoked Trout Deviled Eggs, pipe filling in each individual egg white half and finish with a sprinkling of pepper.

HOMEMADE MAYONNAISE

6 raw egg yolks

2 Tbsp. fresh lemon juice

2 Tbsp. red wine vinegar

2 Tbsp. Dijon mustard

Salt and pepper to taste

2 ½ cups canola oil

1 cup olive oil

2 Tbsp. warm water

Place all ingredients except oils and water in an upright blender and blend until smooth. Incorporate oils in a slow and steady stream until thick. If too thick, add some warm water. Refrigerate for up to three days, covered, until needed.

DEVILED EGG FILLING

12 cooked egg yolks, reserved

1 cup smoked trout, de-skinned and flaked

¾ cup Homemade Mayonnaise

1 Tbsp. lemon juice

½ cup Italian parsley, roughly chopped

Salt and pepper to taste

Place yolks and trout in a food processor and blend until smooth. Add Homemade Mayonnaise and blend until smooth. Finish with lemon juice and seasoning, and then fold in parsley. Place mixture in a piping bag and reserve until needed.

HAM CHIPS

4 thin slices Edwards ham

Preheat oven to 300 degrees. Cut slices of prosciutto/ham into four even pieces. Place ham on a sheet pan lined with a Silpat (silicone baking mat). Bake until crisp, about 20 - 25 minutes. Remove and reserve in an airtight container for up to three days.

FIRE-ROASTED FLAT BREAD

4 pieces flat bread

1 Tbsp. olive oil

Brush flat bread lightly with oil and grill evenly on both sides. Cut into 8 even triangles.

SERVING SUGGESTION:
Present 3 halves of the eggs per person and garnish each with a ham chip. Serve with a side dish of Spicy Hee-Haw pickles and grilled flat bread. Also, serve this delicacy with the Après Cidre cocktail, HANDCRAFTED COCKTAIL section.

SMOKED CHEDDAR & CHORIZO TEQUEÑOS

COPPER CONFERENCE CENTER • CHEF DAVID TALADAY • COPPER MOUNTAIN, COLORADO

The Copper Conference Center is the flagship operation of the Copper Mountain culinary program, as it houses the scratch banquet facility, the scratch bakeshop and the commissary program where signature menu items for the a la carte restaurants are created. Colorado proud, the Copper Conference Center sources local produce, local meats and local specialty items for intimate wedding dinners, an All Natural Organic Farm-to-Table dinner and custom-designed menus for any occasion.

½ lb. fresh chorizo

1 fresh jalapeno, diced

1 fresh corn on the cob

2 Tbsp. cilantro, chopped

8 oz. cooked black beans

1 small white onion, diced

8 oz. whipped cream cheese

6 oz. smoked cheddar cheese, shredded

4 oz. Oaxaca cheese, shredded

Salt and pepper to taste

1 package 7 x 7-inch eggroll wrappers

½ cup water

SERVES 8

Brown chorizo and drain fat. Cool and roughly chop. Lightly season and grill corn on the cob. When cooled, remove kernels. Thoroughly rinse black beans and combine chorizo, jalapeno, corn kernels, black beans and onion. Into mixture, fold Oaxaca cheese, smoked cheddar cheese, whipped cream cheese and cilantro. Mix all ingredients thoroughly. Season to taste with salt and pepper.

Lay out 3 eggroll wrappers and place 2 - 3 oz. of mixture onto each wrapper. Brush the edges with water. Fold over both sides to create the ends of the tequeño. Then, roll the filled wrapper and seal the last flap with a bit of water. Repeat rolling process until finished with chorizo mixture.

Lightly fry for 3 - 4 minutes or until golden brown.

JALAPENO & ONION RELISH

1 red onion, finely julienned

1 large jalapeno, finely julienned

1 tsp. olive oil

1 tsp. white vinegar

1 lime, juiced

2 Tbsp. cilantro, chopped

Salt and pepper to taste

Yields 1 cup

Combine all ingredients into a small bowl. Season to taste with salt and pepper. Mix well. Let rest at room temperature for 30 minutes.

SERVING SUGGESTION:
Serve with Jalapeno and Onion Relish, Chipotle Drizzle and Avocado Sauce. Enjoy these bites with the refreshing Nativa Terra Sangria, HANDCRAFTED COCKTAIL section.

CHIPOTLE DRIZZLE

2 Tbsp. chipotle pepper in adobo sauce, pureed

½ cup sour cream

1 lime, juiced

1 red pepper, roasted

Salt and pepper to taste

Yields 1 ½ cups

Roast, peel and clean red pepper, and then roughly chop. Combine all ingredients into a blender and puree until smooth. Season with salt and pepper.

AVOCADO SAUCE

1 large avocado

1 Tbsp. olive oil

1 lime, juiced

¼ cup sour cream

Salt and pepper to taste

Yields 1 cup

Peel and seed avocado. Combine all ingredients in a blender and puree until smooth. Season with salt and pepper to taste.

AHI NACHOS

THE FIRE TOWER RESTAURANT & TAVERN • CHEF MAX TURNER • STRATTON, VERMONT

With an unparalleled local pride, The Fire Tower Restaurant and Tavern - named after the iconic fire tower that sits atop Stratton Mountain - showcases locally milled timbers, barn board expertly installed by local Vermont craftsmen and custom lighting hand-blown by friends at Manchester Hot Glass. Not to be outdone by its ambiance, the culinary treasures include classic comfort fare inspired by Vermont artisans, as well as some of the most unique Vermont craft beer selections.

3 cups canola oil

12 oz. wonton skins or egg roll wrappers

6 oz. 1+ sushi grade Ahi tuna

¼ cup ponzu sauce

¼ cup hoisin sauce

⅜ cup wasabi cream

1 Tbsp. pea or radish sprouts

2 Tbsp. Pickled Red Onions

2 Tbsp. daikon or red radish, thinly sliced

Serves **4**

 MORE DIFFICULT

Cut dough into diagonal triangles (halved for wonton skins, quartered for eggroll wrappers). Heat oil in high-sided pan until 375 degrees. Add triangles, making sure to separate them. Stir with a slotted spoon or skimmer, so that all triangles become brown and crisp. Remove from oil and drain on a sheet tray with a paper towel underneath to absorb excess oil. Allow to stand at room temperature until needed. You can make ahead and store in an airtight, dry container.

Dice chilled Ahi tuna into ¼-inch cubes. Toss Ahi cubes with ponzu sauce and allow to sit for 10 minutes in the refrigerator. Pile crisp triangles in a shallow bowl or rimmed platter. Gently scatter Ahi cubes over triangles. Using ladles or squeeze bottles, splash the wasabi cream and hoisin sauce over the cubes, reserve 10% of each. Break up and spread pea shoots over the top, as well as the onions and radish shavings. Carrots, cucumber and/or parsnips can also be peeled and finely diced to add crunch and flavor to your own version of Ahi Nachos. Finally, drizzle remaining wasabi cream and hoisin over the top.

PICKLED RED ONIONS

1 red onion, finely diced

½ cup fresh lime juice

Pinch sea salt

Mix onion with lime juice and sea salt. Rest for 1 hour. Drain thoroughly.

WASABI CREAM

½ cup mayonnaise

½ cup sour cream

4 tsp. wasabi powder

3 tsp. pickled ginger juice

¾ cup pickled ginger

½ cucumber, peeled and seeded

1 tsp. sugar

Hot water

Combine wasabi and sugar with enough hot water to make a slurry paste. Then, pulse in a processor with remaining ingredients until smooth.

SERVING SUGGESTION:
To celebrate the Vermont local scene, enjoy these nachos with a Vermont craft beer,
such as Switchback Ale or Long Trail Ale.

BITES & NIBBLES   21

MINI PORK CHEEK TACOS

AVALANCHE PUB AT VAIL MARRIOTT MOUNTAIN RESORT • VAIL, COLORADO

If you are looking for a great spot for après ski libations and nibbles in Vail, Avalanche Pub in Vail Village is the place. Enjoy light hors d'oeuvres, like the Mini Pork Cheek Tacos, and cocktails by the warmth of the fireplace.

5 lbs. pork cheek, cleaned

3 Tbsp. oil

2 stalks celery, chopped

2 carrots, chopped

1 yellow onion, chopped

3 cloves garlic, chopped

2 quarts Pepsi

2 bay leaves

2 sprigs thyme

Salt and pepper to taste

5 double-stacked (10 total) mini corn tortillas

Poblano Cream

Pico

Pickled Cabbage

Cotija cheese, shredded

Cilantro leaves

SERVES 2

MORE DIFFICULT

For the pork, heat oil in a heavy bottomed pot and season cleaned pork cheeks with salt and black pepper. Sear the cheeks until golden on all sides, and add the vegetables. Cook until wilted. Add Pepsi, bay leaves and thyme; boil and reduce heat. Braise for 3 hours or until pork is falling apart.

To assemble, heat corn tortillas and fill with braised pork cheek and Poblano Cream. Top with Pico, Pickled Cabbage, shredded Cotija cheese and fresh cilantro.

POBLANO CREAM

1 large Poblano pepper, roasted and cleaned

½ lime, juiced

¼ tsp. cumin

Salt and pepper to taste

Sour cream

Process all ingredients together and adjust seasoning with salt and pepper.

PICKLED CABBAGE

4 cups cabbage, shredded

1 cup water

¼ cup rice wine vinegar

2 Tbsp. sugar

2 tsp. salt

2 tsp. cumin

Simmer water, vinegar, sugar, salt and cumin until all seasonings are dissolved. Let cool and pour over shredded cabbage.

PICO

1 large ripe tomato, small diced

½ red onion, small diced

½ jalapeno, diced with seeds

¼ bunch cilantro, chopped

Fresh lime juice to taste

Salt and pepper to taste

Mix first 4 ingredients together and season to taste with the lime, salt and pepper.

SERVING SUGGESTION:
Serve tacos with a lime wedge for a sprinkle of tartness.

PARMESAN TRUFFLE FRIES

CHAIR 9 AT THE LITTLE NELL • ASPEN, COLORADO

Parmesan Truffle Fries are a staple and quintessential après contribution from Chair 9 at The Little Nell. Truffle oil and freshly grated Parmesan Reggiano elevates traditional French fries for the sophisticated skier.

Kennebec potatoes, or your choice of potato

Flat-leaf parsley, finely chopped

Parmesan Reggiano cheese, micro planed or finely grated

White truffle oil

Salt and pepper to taste

SERVES DESIRED PARTY SIZE

EASIEST

Wash potatoes and slice into fry-shape. Fry potatoes at 375 degrees until crispy; drain. Drizzle with truffle oil and add parsley, cheese and salt and pepper to your liking.

SERVING SUGGESTION:
Enjoy these fries with the delicious Chair 9 Yard Sale cocktail, HANDCRAFTED COCKTAIL section.

BANGERS WITH SWEDISH MASHERS

STEIN ERIKSEN LODGE • CHEF ZANE HOLMQUIST • PARK CITY, UTAH

Bangers with Swedish Mashers is a traditional European dish made of sausages and mashed potatoes. An example of "pub grub," this dish is relatively easy and quick to make, even in large quantities. To elevate this dish, you may use more exotic, flavored sausages made of pork, beef and/or Cumberland sausage.

Sausages, your preference

6 - 8 medium Yukon Gold potatoes

½ rutabaga

½ parsnip

1 Tbsp. salt for cooking water

½ cup cream

3 Tbsp. butter

1 Tbsp. kosher salt

½ tsp. white pepper

¼ tsp. nutmeg

SERVES 6 — 8

EASIEST

To create the Swedish Mashers, start by removing cream from refrigerator and set aside. Peel and quarter potatoes, peel and largely dice rutabaga and parsnip (parsnip and rutabaga pieces should be half the size of the potato pieces).

Place potatoes, rutabaga and parsnip in an 8-quart saucepan and cover with salted water. Simmer for about 25 minutes or until vegetables are soft. Drain in a colander and let them sit in the colander for 2 - 3 minutes. Process the potato mixture through a food mill or ricer. Add the room temperature cream, butter, salt, pepper and nutmeg to the processed potatoes and gently stir, being careful not to over-mix. Hold the potatoes warm until serving. Heat your sausages—you may serve these whole or sliced.

SERVING SUGGESTION:

Serve bangers (sausages) and mashers (mashed potatoes) together for a warm-up after a chilly day on the mountain.

CHEESY ARTICHOKE DIP

THE PICKLE BARREL • CHEF SHARON ZIMMERMAN • SILVERTON, COLORADO

Cheesy Artichoke Dip is truly enjoyed by many-a-skier after a hard day on the mountain. This tremendously easy, creamy and hearty dip is decadent on buttery crackers or homemade baguette bread.

2 cans diced artichokes

2 small tomatoes, diced

½ cup Caesar dressing

½ cup mayo

½ cup sour cream

¼ cup Parmesan cheese, shredded

½ cup Swiss cheese, diced

2—3 splashes Frank's Red Hot Sauce

SERVES 4 - 6

EASIEST

Mix all ingredients together and put in a baking dish. (When selecting a hot sauce, use your preference, although Tabasco doesn't work well with this recipe.) Bake at 350 degrees for 30 minutes, let sit and then serve.

SERVING SUGGESTION:
Serve the dip with an assortment of crackers and vegetables or homemade baguettes for your dipping preference.

SHRIMP & AVOCADO DIP
with Blue Corn Chips

SILVER FORK LODGE AND RESTAURANT • BRIGHTON, UTAH

Great for springtime après ski or a summertime party, Silver Fork Lodge and Restaurant offers the "totally addicting" Shrimp and Avocado Dip with Blue Corn Chips. Even more perfect is the suggestion of pairing this with the Bartender's Margarita to create a delicious and easy combination—an absolute crowd-pleaser!

1 lb. shrimp, cooked and cut into small chunks

2 avocados, chopped

4 jalapenos, seeded and diced

1 tomato, diced

½ onion, diced

½ bunch of cilantro, diced

1 cup fresh lime juice

Salt and pepper to taste

Sprinkle cayenne (optional, depending on the level of heat desired)

SERVES 10

Combine all ingredients. Serve with blue corn chips.

SERVING SUGGESTION:
Pair this addicting dip with Silver Fork Lodge's Bartender's Margarita, HANDCRAFTED COCKTAIL section.

SRIRACHA & MOLASSES CHICKEN WINGS

SLIDERS RESTAURANT AT THE JORDAN HOTEL • NEWRY, MAINE

The Jordan Hotel, a premier address at Sunday River Resort, offers sweeping views across the valley. Located at the base of the resort's Jordan Bowl area, Sliders is a perfect après spot—featuring entertainment and a great place to relax and unwind after a tremendous day on the hill.

8 chicken wings

Sliders' Wing Sauce

Blue cheese dressing

SERVES 1—2

EASIEST

Salt each chicken wing. Deep-fry until crispy and cooked throughout. Drain and cool, then toss the wings in Sliders' Wing Sauce. Serve with blue cheese dressing.

SLIDERS' WING SAUCE

17 oz. bottle Sriracha

⅜ cup molasses

2 cups ketchup

⅜ cup maple syrup

1 cup butter, melted and cooled

Combine all ingredients.

SERVING SUGGESTION:

Serve the wings with blue cheese dressing and enjoy them with the Jordan Bloody Mary, HANDCRAFTED COCKTAIL section.

CHILI CON QUESO

TAVERN ON THE SQUARE AT THE ARRABELLE AT VAIL SQUARE •
CHEF DOUGLAS DODD • VAIL, COLORADO

Tavern on the Square is famous for creations such as Buffalo Meatloaf, Honey Lacquered Duck and Grilled Elk Quesadilla to name a few. If diners' tastes are more traditional, American classics like St. Louis style BBQ Ribs or Build Your Own Macaroni and Cheese are other tried-and-true options. But, an absolute favorite of locals and out-of-towners is the Chili Con Queso with soft pretzels—a must sample!

½ lb. chorizo sausage

1 cup whole milk

1 cup American cheese, shredded

½ cup cheddar cheese, shredded

½ cup pepper jack cheese, shredded

1 Tbsp. all purpose flour

¼ cup pico de gallo (chunky salsa may be substituted)

1 tsp. chili powder

4 Tbsp. canned green chilies

1 Tbsp. Sambal Chili Paste

Tortilla chips

Soft pretzels

SERVES 4

 MORE DIFFICULT

Remove casings from sausage and break sausage into little pieces. In a thick saucepan, brown chorizo until cooked. Add milk and gently warm. Toss cheeses with the flour and gradually add cheese mixture to warm milk and chorizo. Continue stirring over low heat until cheese melts. Remove from heat. Fold in pico de gallo, chili powder, green chilies and chili paste. Season with more or less chili paste to desired heat. Keep warm.

Brush soft pretzels with butter and warm. Sprinkle with pretzel salt, once warmed.

SERVING SUGGESTION:
Dip is best served in a warm fondue pot. Serve with warm and fresh tortilla chips and prepared soft pretzels.

WORLD FAMOUS CHOW-CHOW

STEIN ERIKSEN LODGE • CHEF ZANE HOLMQUIST • PARK CITY, UTAH

Deer Valley Resort offers a welcome concept of combining first-class services, luxury accommodations and gourmet food with skiing and is consistently in the #1 rankings for service, grooming and on-mountain food by the readers of Ski Magazine.

½ head green cabbage, julienned

½ cucumber, peeled and julienned

2 medium onions, julienned

½ habanero pepper, julienned

1 Tbsp. kosher salt

1 Tbsp. black pepper

3 Tbsp. turmeric

1 Tbsp. coriander

1 tsp. celery seed

1 Tbsp. mustard seed

1 Tbsp. kosher salt

1 tsp. red chili flakes

4 bay leaves

1 cup champagne vinegar

¼ cup white wine

½ cup sugar

SERVES 4 - 6

EASIEST

Combine cabbage, cucumber, onion and pepper in a bowl. Add salt and pepper; let this mixture sit overnight in the refrigerator. Combine the remaining ingredients in a saucepan. Simmer for 15 minutes. Pour this mixture over the vegetables and stir well. Let cool and serve. This will keep 2 - 3 weeks refrigerated.

SERVING SUGGESTION:
Serve this different take on coleslaw either cooled or warmed.

WINTER SQUASH PORRIDGE

MANZANITA AT RITZ CARLTON • TRUCKEE, CALIFORNIA

The menu at Manzanita features California cuisine, with a regional mountain resort influence, and sourcing of organic, sustainable and locally grown meats and produce. From the moment you enter the restaurant, the design radiates warmth, texture and natural materials with an open kitchen, visible from all vantage points in the restaurant.

1 butternut squash

⅓ Tbsp. olive oil

2 sprigs thyme

1 cup cream

Black pepper to taste, coarsely cracked

Kosher salt to taste

Brown sugar to taste

S ERVES 4

 MORE DIFFICULT

Preheat oven to 300 degrees. Cut squash in half and remove seeds with a spoon. Season squash with salt, pepper, olive oil and thyme. Place on cookie sheet with parchment paper, flesh side down. Bake for 40 minutes or until soft. Remove from oven, and scrape out flesh and place in a saucepan. Add cream and cook for 30 - 45 minutes on low-medium heat. Pour mixture into a blender; add salt and sugar to taste and blend until smooth. Allow mixture to cool.

GRITS

2 cups Anson Mills white corn meal

1 quart milk

2 cups cream

2 cups vegetable stock

½ lb. butter

Salt to taste

Melt butter in a saucepan. Add milk, cream, vegetable stock and salt. Cook to a simmer. Slowly add grits while whisking. Let cook on medium heat for 4 minutes, constantly stirring. Turn heat to very low and cook until grits are very soft, whisking every 4 - 5 minutes.

SERVING SUGGESTION:
Add one part squash puree to two parts grits and garnish with honey and freshly cracked black pepper.

CARAMELIZED BRUSSEL SPROUTS
with Soy-Chili Vinaigrette

ZACH'S TAVERN AT THE HYDE AWAY INN • WAITSFIELD, VERMONT

Zach's Tavern at The Hyde Away Inn offers farm-to-table dining with just a little more ... The little more takes place in a casual, unpretentious, truly relaxing environment with the amazingly talented kitchen staff preparing New American cuisine with a focus on using the freshest ingredients.

2 lbs. brussel sprouts, halved

Soy - Chili Vinaigrette

SERVES 10

EASIEST

Roast sprouts in a 350-degree oven for 30 - 45 minutes until golden brown. This can be done ahead of time and refrigerated for 2 days. Warm sprouts by sautéing for 3 - 4 minutes until softened and warm. Add vinaigrette and sauté for 2 ½ - 3 minutes longer. Serve right away.

SOY - CHILI VINAIGRETTE

⅓ cup fish sauce

¼ cup water

2 Tbsp. rice wine vinegar

¼ cup sugar

1 garlic clove, chopped

½ tsp. chili paste

Mix together all ingredients to make vinaigrette.

SERVING SUGGESTION:
Serve alongside the palette-pleasing Mason Maple Shandy cocktail, HANDCRAFTED COCKTAIL section.

SWEET CHILI SAUCE FOR WINGS

CHAIR 9 AT THE LITTLE NELL • ASPEN, COLORADO

In this recipe, a term is used that is very familiar to BBQ enthusiasts. To improve a BBQ, a good "mop" is a step to try. A "mop" is a thin, basting sauce that is used during cooking, usually a slow smoking. It adds flavor and keeps the meat from getting dry.

Chicken wings

Sweet Chili Wing Sauce

SERVES DESIRED PARTY SIZE

EASIEST

Bake chicken wings at a low temperature. Do not apply the "mop" more than once every 30 minutes, and be quick to get the door closed so temperature does not drop too much.

SWEET CHILI WING SAUCE

51 fl. oz. Mae Ploy sweet chili sauce

6 oz. Ginger Lime Vinegar

1 Tbsp. ground coriander

Combine all ingredients to create the "mop."

GINGER LIME VINEGAR

¾ lb. sugar

½ quart rice wine vinegar

¾ lb. ginger, peeled and roughly chopped

¼ quart lime juice

Combine sugar, vinegar and ginger in a medium saucepot. Bring to a simmer, stirring to dissolve the sugar and turn off the heat. Steep for 30 minutes, then cool in an ice bath. When the liquid is cool, stir in the lime juice to finish the vinegar.

SERVING SUGGESTION:
Garnish these moist wings with chopped cilantro.

TWO CHEESE FONDUE WITH KIRSCH

FORMERLY OF JOHN'S ANGELS CATERING • LAKESIDE, MONTANA

The Two Cheese Fondue with Kirsch was a dish created for John's Angels cooking class. Fondue is a fun appetizer to share with friends, as well as a great way to socialize with strangers. This pairs well with wine and beer from Tamarack Brewing Company.

1 block Gruyere cheese, shredded

1 block Manchego cheese, shredded

1 ½ - 2 cups white wine, preferably not chardonnay

Kirsch to taste

1 Tbsp. flour

½ - 1 Tbsp. Louisiana Hot Sauce

4 dashes truffle oil

Salt and pepper to taste

SERVES 6 - 8

EASIEST

Place the shredded cheese into a Ziploc bag with flour and shake well to coat. Bring white wine and Kirsch to a boil and reduce to low. Slowly add handfuls of cheese and stir in a figure-eight pattern until melted. Only add the amount of cheese for your desired batch consistency—to test, dip a mushroom and the cheese should stay on the vegetable. If it does not, add more cheese. Add Louisiana Hot Sauce, depending on the heat level desired. Add truffle oil and salt and pepper to taste.

SERVING SUGGESTION:
Enjoy the fondue with mushrooms, carrots, celery, broccoli, pretzel sticks, sweet bread (white and dark), cooked tenderloin tips and/or any other desired items.

KASSERI:
Greek Cheese Flamed Tableside

CARBON COUNTY STEAKHOUSE • CHEF ERIC TRAGER • RED LODGE, MONTANA

The Carbon County Steakhouse's featured appetizer, Kasseri—Greek cheese, flamed tableside with Sambuca liquer, has been a unique favorite since the Grand Opening of the restaurant in 2000. This traditional Greek cheese is made primarily from sheep's milk and is delicious when paired with a fruity, bright and intense, yet finely balanced Zinfandel, like the Ancient Peaks Zinfandel.

Kasseri cheese, grated

Breadcrumbs, unseasoned

1 oz. Sambuca Liqueur

½ oz. 151 Bacardi Rum

Lemon wedge

Flat bread, grilled

S ERVES **4**

EASIEST

Heat a small cast iron skillet in a 400-degree oven. Add grated kasseri cheese, 1-inch in depth. Top with a heavy layer of breadcrumbs. Bake for 10 minutes or until completely melted, and remove from oven.

Drizzle Sambuca Liqueur and 151 Bacardi Rum on top, then flame, allowing flame to completely burnout. Squeeze juice from fresh lemon wedge and serve with grilled flat bread.

SERVING SUGGESTION:
Enjoy alongside an Espresso Martini, HANDCRAFTED COCKTAIL section.

ENOTECA WOOD-OVEN ROASTED BACON BRUSSEL SPROUTS
with Goat Cheese Aioli

ENOTECA RESTAURANT AND WINE BAR • CHEF SCOTT MASON • KETCHUM, IDAHO

Brussel sprouts are an old favorite with Ketchum locals and visitors, especially accompanied with bacon. Enoteca serves a version of these favorites year-round. The goat cheese aioli was recently introduced and is a very tasty addition.

20 large brussel sprouts, quartered from top to bottom

4 strips wood-smoked bacon, coarsely chopped

2 Tbsp. olive oil

Kosher salt

Black pepper

Goat Cheese Aioli

SERVES 4

MORE DIFFICULT

Sauté bacon in a large sauté pan over medium heat until it begins to render some of its fat. Add brussel sprouts, toss with bacon and season with salt and pepper. Place in a preheated 500-degree oven for 10 minutes or until bacon is crisp and brussel sprouts have cooked to roasted brown color. Remove from oven and spoon from pan onto a serving platter being careful to leave any extra cooking fat behind. Serve with Goat Cheese Aioli drizzled over the top or as a dipping sauce.

GOAT CHEESE AIOLI

3 Tbsp. Dijon mustard

1 egg yolk

¼ cup lemon juice

1 cup virgin olive oil

2 oz. fresh goat cheese

3 garlic cloves

Place all ingredients in a 2-cup container. Using an immersion blender, gradually emulsify all ingredients into a smooth aioli.

SERVING SUGGESTION:
Adelaide Mason, manager at Enoteca, suggests pairing these sprouts with the bubbly Italian Kir Royale cocktail, HANDCRAFTED COCKTAIL section.

SPRING ROLLS

FORKLIFT RESTAURANT • SNOWBIRD, UTAH

Conveniently located in Snowbird on the Plaza Deck across from the Tram, Forklift Restaurant guests can enjoy après ski fare during the winter. Dishing up hearty fare for over 30 years and nestled slopeside among tall pines, The Forklift is a Snowbird family dining favorite.

2 cups rice noodles

1 tsp. salt

1 Tbsp. fresh mint leaves, chopped

1 Tbsp. fresh basil leaves, chopped

1 cup carrots, shredded

12 cucumber slices, thinly sliced

12 fresh cilantro leaves

Rice paper wraps

Red leaf lettuce

Peanut Sauce

SERVES 4

 In a large soup pot, boil 3 quarts of water and salt. Add rice noodles and cook for 15 minutes. Drain hot water and run rice noodles under cold water until cooled. Drain. Toss noodles with mint and basil.

Wet rice paper wrap with room temperature water. Place ¼ cup noodles in middle of rice wrap. Top with 1 Tbsp. shredded carrots, 2 cucumber slices and a cilantro leaf on top of each cucumber. Wrap rice paper burrito-style around noodles. Arrange spring rolls on a bed of red leaf lettuce, as garnish.

PEANUT SAUCE

1 ½ cups crunchy peanut butter

¼ cup rice vinegar

¼ cup soy sauce

3 Tbsp. water

3 Tbsp. lime juice

3 Tbsp. red chili paste

2 Tbsp. garlic, chopped

1 Tbsp. brown sugar

2 tsp. hoisin sauce

Combine all ingredients in a blender and mix until smooth.

SERVING SUGGESTION:
Serve the spring rolls with a side of Peanut Sauce. Also, the spring rolls taste extra special with the Ginger Joy cocktail, HANDCRAFTED COCKTAIL section.

SPICY DUCK NINJA ROLL

CHARLIE B'S PUB AND RESTAURANT • STOWE, VERMONT

At Stoweflake Mountain Resort and Spa, you can eat and drink at Charlie B's Pub and Restaurant. Charlie B's Pub is a Stowe tradition with a festive, fireside dining atmosphere, Vermont-fresh cuisine, live entertainment and an award-winning wine list of over 50 wines by the glass, as well as a martini bar and ten beers on tap. The Vermont-style decor features a cozy, friendly bar, high-back booths and Baraw family ski memorabilia.

1 sheet seaweed paper, like Nori

¾ cup sushi rice, prepared

½ cup duck confit, finely chopped

2 Tbsp. Sriracha (Chinese hot sauce)

2 Tbsp. miso aioli

1 tsp. rice wine vinegar

1 tsp. sugar

Pickled ginger

Seaweed salad

Salt and pepper to taste

Flour to dust roll

Tempura batter

SERVES 2

In a bowl, combine prepared sushi rice with vinegar and sugar. Toss until the rice has cooled. In another bowl, combine duck confit with 1 Tbsp. Sriracha, 1 Tbsp. miso aioli, salt and pepper. Dip fingers in the water before you handle the rice, and then spread the rice mixture three-quarters over the Nori paper, leaving ¼-inch strip on the top to seal. Make a line with the duck confit mixture one-third from the bottom of the roll. Roll from bottom to the top, dampening the end with water to make it stick. Cut the roll in half and dust with a little bit of flour. Dip in tempura batter and cook in a deep fryer for 2 minutes. With the remaining Sriracha and miso aioli, make 7 lines with each on a plate in a crisscross pattern. Cut the roll into 7 equal pieces and lay on top of the sauces.

SERVING SUGGESTION:
Garnish with pickled ginger and seaweed salad. Accompany with the Ginger-tini, HANDCRAFTED COCKTAIL section.

CHARRED JALAPEÑO WHITE BEAN PUREE

CHIMNEY ROCK GRILLE • CHEF KELLEY KENNEDY • SANDPOINT, IDAHO

Embracing patrons' dietary restrictions, Chimney Rock Grille created a tasty, gluten-free and dairy-free appetizer for all to enjoy, including vegetarians and vegans. Even the most meat-devoted clientele are enjoying this recipe. To achieve a sweeter, less spicy dip, substitute non-spicy items for the jalapeños, like sweet Peppadews or a favorite savory herb, like rosemary. Keeping the base the same, this recipe is served at Chimney Rock Grille as a trio with sweet Peppadew, fiery jalapeño and savory rosemary-roasted garlic.

2 15 oz. cans white beans (any white bean, Cannellini, Great Northern, etc.)

½ lemon, zested and juiced

Pinch white pepper

1 tsp. kosher salt

2 garlic cloves

4 Tbsp. olive oil

1 jalapeño, charred

SERVES 4

 EASIEST

Place garlic cloves and olive oil in a small saucepan, then roast the garlic cloves to golden brown over low heat. Reserve the oil and set both garlic and oil aside. Evenly char the jalapeño over an open flame, typically on a grill or with the flame from a gas burner. This can also be done in the oven on broil. Once charred, pull stem and chop into 3 pieces; set aside. Wash spicy jalapeño oils off hands.

Place white beans in a strainer, rinse and drain. In a food processor with the blade attachment or in a high power blender, add all ingredients except reserved olive oil from cooking the garlic. Blend until ingredients start to incorporate together. Drizzle in reserved oil a little bit at a time until desired texture (smooth dip texture, like hummus) is achieved. Serve with corn tortilla chips and sliced vegetables.

SERVING SUGGESTION:
As this dip can be quite spicy (depending on the jalapeño), refresh your taste buds with the Icy Coconut Cosmo, HANDCRAFTED COCKTAIL section.

SNOWBASIN NACHOS

CINNABAR • HUNTSVILLE, UTAH

Located inside Earl's Lodge at the base of Snowbasin Resort, Cinnabar is the best place to unwind and talk about your day on the mountain in the comfort and convenience of a slope-side restaurant lounge, but without pretention. Cinnabar is known for its live music, mouth-watering appetizers, unbelievable lunches, friendly service and fun for everyone. For those looking for a little more adventure in their après ski or lunch experience, Cinnabar has a shot-ski, a beer sampler ski and the hottest wings west of the Mississippi.

5 oz. kettle-cooked potato chips

4 oz. chicken, cooked, smoked and diced

2 oz. bacon crumbles, cooked

4 oz. warm Blue Cheese Fondue

2 oz. cheddar cheese, shredded

SERVES 2

Place potato chips in a large bowl or on a platter. Top with chicken and bacon crumbles. Smother with Blue Cheese Fondue and shredded cheddar cheese, then put under the broiler until cheddar cheese starts to caramelize.

BLUE CHEESE FONDUE

2 cups butter

2 cups all purpose flour

2 garlic cloves, minced

1 shallot, minced

¼ tsp. thyme

12 oz. bottle Hefeweizen beer

2 cups chicken stock

1 ½ cups cream

1 lb. blue cheese

2 dashes Tabasco sauce

1 Tbsp. honey

1 tsp. lemon juice

In large saucepan, sauté garlic, shallots and thyme in butter. Stir flour into melted butter to make roux. Mix cream, beer and chicken stock into the roux until no lumps remain. Simmer and cook for 15 minutes, stirring occasionally on medium heat. Mixture should start to thicken, then stir in Tabasco sauce, honey and lemon juice. Mix in blue cheese and let cook on low heat for 15 minutes, stirring occasionally.

SERVING SUGGESTION:
Garnish with green onions, sour cream and diced tomatoes. Enjoy with Basin Connection Cocoa 2.0, HANDCRAFTED COCKTAIL section.

WARM ONION TART

THE FARM • PARK CITY, UTAH

Recently, The Farm was named the "Best New Restaurant" in Utah by Salt Lake Magazine *and offers fresh, prepared from scratch, sustainably raised fare. Whenever possible, The Farm strives to source from local farms and purveyors. Located in the heart of the Resort Village and overlooking the Ski Beach, this rustic yet refined restaurant offers both indoor and outdoor dining and features a welcoming lounge with an amazing selection of wines and cocktails for your après appetite.*

1 sheet frozen puff pastry, thawed

2 lbs. yellow onions, sliced into rings

2 sprigs fresh thyme

2 eggs

½ cup half and half

5 strips bacon, diced

2 Tbsp. olive oil

2 Tbsp. butter

1 tsp. salt

2 tsp. freshly ground black pepper

S ERVES **4 - 6**

EASIEST

Heat large sauté pan on medium heat, melt butter and oil together in a large skillet and add diced bacon. Cook until the bacon is halfway cooked. Add thyme, onion and salt to the skillet. Reduce heat to medium-low and cook until the onions are completely translucent and caramelized. This will take approximately 30 minutes. Remove from heat and cool slightly.

Combine eggs and half and half in a bowl. Add the caramelized onion mixture and the freshly ground black pepper. Roll out the puff pastry in a buttered pie or glass dish, making sure the pastry has four edges in order to hold the onion mixture. Add the mixture to the pastry and bake for 35 minutes or until the crust and top are slightly browned. Cool.

SIMPLE ARUGULA SALAD

2 cups fresh arugula

¼ lemon, juiced

2 Tbsp. olive oil

Salt and cracked pepper
to taste

Toss arugula with lemon and olive oil in a bowl. Season with salt and pepper.

SERVING SUGGESTION:
Serve onion tart with a simple arugula salad and alongside The Geoffery cocktail,
HANDCRAFTED COCKTAIL section.

CROSTINI BARBABIETOLE
with Beets, Gorgonzola & Chopped Walnuts

THE BLONDE BEAR TAVERN • CHEF JON MUDDER • TAOS SKI VALLEY, NEW MEXICO

Crostini are grilled, toasted, roasted or fried small crusts of bread capped or smeared with various toppings. The toppings are typically savory, including vegetables, cheeses, pâtés and meats. Crostini are ubiquitous appetizers across Italy and are perfect for Après Ski. The founders of Taos Ski Valley were mostly Alpine European and accordingly, The Blonde Bear Tavern's menu pays homage to its heritage and proudly features Crostini Barbabietole on its menu. These deeply satisfying winter crostini exemplify an iconic flavor affinity found in the northern mountainous regions of Italy. The warming influence of earthy roasted beets is offset by the creamy coolness of Gorgonzola then rounded by the walnuts' astringent tannins and crunch. The result is an equilibrium of flavors and textures.

Fresh baguette loaf, sliced

¼ cup beets

¼ cup Gorgonzola, crumbled (see Note)

¼ cup walnuts, finely chopped

Walnut oil

Sea salt

SERVES **4**

 EASIEST

Preheat oven to 350 degrees. Cut off the tops of the beets at the base of the stems and trim the root ends of the beet bulbs. Wash the beets in cold water, then individually wrap them with foil and place on a sheet pan. Place the sheet pan in the upper part of the oven. Beets are fully cooked when they feel tender, but firm when tested with a knife, about 2 ½ - 3 hours, depending on their size.

Over medium heat, toast chopped walnuts in a skillet (without any oil), shaking the pan occasionally to prevent scorching. Walnuts are done when they begin to darken slightly in color, about 3 - 5 minutes.

While beets are warm, but cool enough to handle, pull off their skins with your fingers, or use a vegetable peeler or the back edge of a paring knife. Hold the beets with a kitchen towel to avoid staining your fingers. Then, chop the beets into ¼-inch cubes and chop Gorgonzola into cubes that match that size (if using crumbled gorgonzola, match the size of the beets).

Note: There are two types of gorgonzola cheese: gorgonzola piccante (also called gorgonzola naturale, gorgonzola montagna or mountain gorgonzola), which is what is used in this recipe, and gorgonzola dolce (also called sweet gorgonzola), a creamier version, which would not work as well.

Chop walnuts finely. Cut 8 slices of bread from baguette about ³/₈-inch per slice and lightly toast the sliced bread. Place about 1 tsp. (depending on size of bread slice) of crumbled gorgonzola on each bread slice, using your fingers to press the cheese onto the bread. On top of the cheese, place about 1 tsp. of chopped beets, then top with the chopped walnuts. Finally, drizzle each crostino with a few drops of walnut oil and sprinkle sea salt on each.

SERVING SUGGESTION:
The Blonde Bear Tavern's sommelier pairs these crostini with wine; either a white Roero Arneis or a low-tannin red Barbera, both from Piedmont. Also, you can enjoy this with a Taos Sunset, HANDCRAFTED COCKTAIL section.

TUNA NACHOS

158 MAIN • CHEF JACK FOLEY • JEFFERSONVILLE, VERMONT

158 Main has a menu that combines the traditional and the new, which has succeeded in bringing a loyal local following in a community that is a mix of families who have been there for generations, long-time transplants and new arrivals. Depending on when you visit, you will notice businessmen, friends, family, art aficionados or avid skiers enjoying their meals—once they've met that first challenge of making a choice off the menu.

3 wonton wrappers

Asian Slaw

Ponzu

Pepper, freshly ground

5 oz. sushi grade Ahi tuna

SERVES 2

 MORE DIFFICULT Fry wonton wrappers until crisp. (You can place them between two pizza screens and clamp to hold, then submerge into a fryer for approximately 1 minute.) Mix together Asian Slaw and some Ponzu and place on each wonton. Dust tuna with pepper and sear both sides in a hot sauté pan for 15 seconds on each side. Slice tuna steak and place on slaw. Arrange on a plate and serve with more Ponzu for dipping.

SERVING SUGGESTION:
Garnish nachos with wasabi and Sriracha. Enjoy these with the Après Main cocktail, HANDCRAFTED COCKTAIL section.

ASIAN SLAW

Napa cabbage, shredded

Carrots, julienned

Red pepper, julienned

Green onions, small diced

Assemble all ingredients together.

PONZU

3 Tbsp. hoisin

3 Tbsp. sweet chili sauce

3 Tbsp. soy sauce

2 tsp. fresh garlic, minced

2 tsp. fresh ginger, minced

Mix together all ingredients.

FRENCHED DRUMSTICKS

Enjoy the après ski scene with live music at the longest bar in Summit County. Serving lunch and dinner, JJ's Rocky Mountain Tavern is a turn-of-the-century tavern based on the legacy of historical figures JJ and Molly Brown. To show evidence of some of the best slow-smoked BBQ around, Chef Jeff shares the Frenched Drumstick recipe.

3 lbs. drumsticks

Spice Rub

Raspberry Chipotle Sauce

SERVES 8 - 10

MORE DIFFICULT

Grasp fat end of drumstick with one hand and, using a small sharp knife, cut drumstick at the base of the muscle to remove all skin and tendons on the "handle" of the drumstick down to bare bone. Dredge with spice rub and bake in a 250-degree oven for about 50 minutes, depending on the size of your drumsticks and how crisp you like them. Allow to cool slightly and toss in Raspberry Chipotle Sauce.

SERVING SUGGESTION:
Enjoy the drummies with the Perfect Raspberry Lemonade Cocktail, HANDCRAFTED COCKTAIL section.

SPICE RUB

⅛ cup brown sugar

⅛ cup dark chili powder

1 Tbsp. black pepper

1 Tbsp. onion powder

1 Tbsp. garlic powder

1 Tbsp. salt

Combine all ingredients.

RASPBERRY CHIPOTLE SAUCE

3 ½ oz. chipotle peppers in adobo sauce (half of a 7 oz. can)

1 ½ cups raspberry preserves

1 cup fresh raspberries

3 Tbsp. honey

3 Tbsp. red wine vinegar

In a medium saucepan, combine all ingredients and simmer about 20 minutes.

CLUB CAR CRAB DIP

CLUB CAR RESTAURANT • CHEF CHRISTOPHER CICCARELLI • WINTER PARK, COLORADO

The Club Car Restaurant is located at the base of the Mary Jane Territory at Winter Park Resort. Mary Jane is home to big bumps, abundant trees and occasionally, some very sore quads. On any given day, tired skiers lounge in the sun on the Club Car deck, re-fueling and taking a break from Mary Jane's infamous moguls. With great food and a friendly staff, Club Car has been a local favorite, and is the perfect choice for lunch while skiing at Winter Park Resort.

1 lb. crab meat

1 lb. cream cheese, softened

1 cup Parmesan cheese, grated

¼ cup horseradish

2 stalks celery, finely diced

½ red onion, finely diced

1 Tbsp. butter

2 Tbsp. parsley, chopped

½ cup sliced almonds

½ cup Mae Ploy Sweet Chili Sauce (available in Asian section of super market)

1 package egg roll skins/wontons

1 cup vegetable oil

SERVES 6

In a pan over medium heat, sauté celery and onion in butter until soft. In a mixing bowl, combine all ingredients, except almonds, wontons, oil and Mae Ploy sauce. Mix well, and transfer to ungreased casserole dish. Top with almonds and bake at 350 degrees for 20 minutes or until almonds are golden brown. Dip can be made and chilled up to 2 days in advance.

Cut wontons into 3-inch triangles. In a skillet, heat oil to 350 degrees (medium-high heat). Fry wontons in small batches until golden brown, about 3 minutes, and reserve. Place dip and Mae Ploy sauce on plate, surround with fried wontons.

SERVING SUGGESTION:
A glass of Chardonnay or the Alpen Twinkle cocktail, HANDCRAFTED COCKTAIL section, pairs well with this dip.

ITALIAN BRUSCHETTA

MATTERHORN SKI BAR • NEWRY, MAINE

Named "Classic Ski Bar" and "Best Ski Bar USA" by both Ski Magazine *and* Skiing Magazine, *the Matterhorn Ski Bar is a tribute to skiing and a museum of vintage equipment and ski memorabilia. Named for the famous Swiss peak, the classic restaurant and bar was inspired by numerous travels to Italy and Switzerland. The mainstay of the classic menu is the authentic Italian Wood-Fired Brick Oven Pizza, as well as one of the oldest and most popular après ski appetizers—Italian Bruschetta, which is also prepared in their "wood-burning" brick oven.*

2 cups artichoke hearts, chopped

1 cup tomato, diced

¼ cup red onion, diced

½ cup pesto sauce

8 oz. package fresh mozzarella, thinly sliced

4 slices rustic Italian bread, brushed with garlic herb oil

Balsamic vinaigrette glaze

Serves 2

EASIEST

Brush and toast bread under a broiler. Combine first four ingredients in a bowl. Transfer into a baking pan and place mozzarella on top. Bake at 350 degrees for 7 - 9 minutes or until cheese is melted. Place onto toasted bread and drizzle with a balsamic vinaigrette glaze. Delizioso!

SERVING SUGGESTION:
Serve this appetizer with Matterhorn Ski Bar's signature Horny Sicilian cocktail, HANDCRAFTED COCKTAIL section.

JOHNNY CAKES
with Black Bean Salsa

TIMBERS RESTAURANT • CHEF GERRY NOONEY • WAITSFIELD, VERMONT

Timbers Restaurant is fashioned after a 19th-century Vermont round dairy barn. With 6,000 square feet of post and beam construction and 45-foot vaulted ceilings, it's a dining location like no other, with a culinary staff like no other, as well. Chef Gerry Nooney's commitment to the local food movement earned him the Vermont Chef of the Year award by the Vermont Chamber of Commerce and his passion for food is unparalleled.

6 Tbsp. unsalted butter, melted

2 eggs

1 ½ cups buttermilk

¾ cup all purpose flour

1 cup corn meal

1 Tbsp. sugar

1 ½ tsp. baking soda

¼ tsp. salt

1 red pepper, roasted, seeded and diced

1 jalapeño, roasted, seeded and diced

2 ears corn, roasted

1 bunch green onions, chopped

SERVES 6

MORE DIFFICULT

Combine first three ingredients and set aside. Mix together flour, corn meal, sugar, baking soda and salt. Fold dry ingredients into wet ingredients. Finally, incorporate vegetables into batter without over mixing. Make cakes by dropping large spoonfuls onto a hot, greased griddle and flatten slightly with the back of a spoon. When brown, turn and cook the other side.

BLACK BEAN SALSA

16 oz. black beans, cooked

3 tomatoes, roasted and peeled

2 bell peppers, roasted, seeded & peeled

2 jalapeños, roasted

3 Tbsp. lime juice

2 Tbsp. black pepper

½ cup cilantro, chopped

½ cup green onions, chopped

½ Tbsp. cumin

½ Tbsp. coriander

½ Tbsp. paprika

½ Tbsp. chili powder

½ Tbsp. dried oregano

Combine all salsa ingredients and set aside for 20 minutes, or up to 2 days.

SERVING SUGGESTION: Serve Johnny Cakes with a heaping of Black Bean Salsa. Enjoy them with a Clockwork Orange cocktail, HANDCRAFTED COCKTAIL section.

APRICOT & BRIE BRUSCHETTA

COLORFUL COOKING • CHEF TRACY MILLER • VAIL VALLEY, COLORADO

Apricots—a colorful, potassium-rich fruit—decrease muscle cramps by replacing potassium in the body after exercising on the ski slopes. Additionally, apricots are high in beta-carotene and vitamin A, which promote a healthy immune system and help bone growth, reproduction and vision.

½ cup apricot jelly

⅓ cup dried apricots

½ cup pecans, toasted

8 oz. Brie cheese

1 French baguette

2 Tbsp. olive oil

SERVES 4 - 6

EASIEST

Slice baguette into ⅓-inch rounds, about 20 pieces. Then, brush each side of the bread with olive oil. Heat broiler to high and layer bread on a baking sheet; place bread under broiler for 1 - 2 minutes each side, until lightly browned.

Toast whole pecans in a dry sauté pan over medium heat for 7 minutes, then chop. Coarsely chop the dried apricots. Thinly slice cheese to cover most of the toasted round.

Assemble the bruschetta by layering on bread rounds: 1 tsp. apricot jelly, a sprinkle of dried apricot, a slice of Brie and 1 scant tsp. chopped pecans. Then, place bruschetta under broiler for 2 minutes.

SERVING SUGGESTION:
Enjoy the bruschetta slices after a hard day on the mountain.

SWEET FIG TAPENADE

COLORFUL COOKING • CHEF TRACY MILLER • VAIL VALLEY, COLORADO

The creator of Colorful Cooking, Tracy Miller teaches cooking classes and hosts television cooking shows. She states, "I've learned that you want quick, healthy recipes that are filling and taste good. My focus is adding fruits and veggies to a protein to create a dish that enhances the natural flavor of the fruit or veggie while delivering the vitamins, minerals and nutrients that your body needs to function at its best."

½ cup raisins

½ cup golden raisins

12 Kalamata olives

10 Mission figs

2 Tbsp. Cerasuola olive oil or extra virgin olive oil

⅓ cup Italian parsley leaves

2 tsp. red wine vinegar

¼ cup feta cheese

¼ tsp. pepper

⅛ tsp. salt (optional)

SERVES 8 - 10

In a bowl, cover raisins with water and soak for 20 minutes, then drain. Slice stems off figs and chop coarsely. Remove parsley leaves from stems and discard stems.

In a food processor, mix all ingredients except cheese. Pulse to desired consistency and gently stir in cheese when ready to serve.

SERVING SUGGESTION:

Serve on crackers or as a sandwich spread. Sweet Fig Tapenade pairs well with salami, pork and poultry.

BLUE CHEESE CHEESECAKE

LOULA'S CAFÉ • CHEF SHAUN MCCOLLUM • WHITEFISH, MONTANA

Having a restaurant at the base of a ski hill, LouLa's Café feeds a massive amount of skiers from all over the world. Whether going up for some turns or getting done, skiers can't wait to kick off their boots, relax and enjoy delicious food. One of those glorious, après ski menu items is the light, savory, pinnacle of the late afternoon: Blue Cheese Cheesecake. In this, you will enjoy a sample of Chef Shaun McCollum's flourishing and creative culinary talents.

1 ½ Tbsp. butter

1 ¼ cups pecans

8 oz. cream cheese, softened

½ cup sour cream

2 whole eggs

1 ½ Tbsp. all purpose flour

Pinch salt

1 Tbsp. Tabasco sauce

½ cup blue cheese, crumbled

¼ cup green onions, sliced

S ERVES 8

MOST DIFFICULT

Preheat the oven to 350 degrees. Melt 1 Tbsp. butter and use the other ½ Tbsp. to grease the inside of a 7-inch spring form pan. In a food processor, add pecans and melted butter; pulse until almost a paste; it should stick to itself. Place this mixture in the bottom of the spring form pan and press it out to the edges, trying to keep a thin, even layer. Set aside when done.

Using a mixer, add cream cheese, sour cream and salt; mix thoroughly until smooth. Add eggs, one at a time, making sure the first egg is fully blended before adding the second. Still mixing, add flour and mix for 30 seconds, then add blue cheese and hot sauce. Mix for 15 seconds. So filling doesn't turn green, fold in the sliced green onions to the cream cheese mixture.

Tear off one 12 x 12-inch square of tin foil and place it flat on a counter. Place your spring form pan in the center of the tin foil and fold the excess edges up to cover the sides of the pan. Pour the cream cheese filling into the spring form pan. Use a rubber spatula to smooth out filling to have a flat surface for even baking. Place the uncooked cheesecake in a 4—6-inch deep-sided roasting pan. Pour water into the pan until it comes halfway up the sides of the cheesecake pan (make sure water does not leak into the tin foil). Very carefully, place the pan in the oven on the middle rack and bake for 50 minutes. When cheesecake is done, it will not jiggle in the middle when shaken. Remove pan carefully and let cool for 15 minutes and then place in refrigerator for at least 12 hours.

When cheesecake is completely cooled, gently remove from spring form pan and serve whole or cut in wedges.

SERVING SUGGESTION:

Serve with your favorite crackers, toast points and fruit. Also, Chef Shaun suggests enjoying this with a local brew, such as the Wheatfish Hefeweizen from the Great Northern Brewery, or a favorite red wine.

ARTICHOKE DIP

MANGY MOOSE RESTAURANT AND SALOON • JACKSON, WYOMING

At the Mangy Moose Restaurant and Saloon, guests enjoy hearty and affordable breakfasts or lunches in the RMO Cafe. Visit what Forbes Traveler *called "One of the 10 Hottest Après Ski Bars in the World" for a Spicy Margarita while listening to live music on the stage. And, share a delicious dinner with family in the Mangy Moose Restaurant or outside on the covered deck.*

2 cans artichoke hearts, quartered

2 Tbsp. olive oil

¼ cup white wine

1 Tbsp. basil, chopped

2 tsp. fresh thyme, chopped

2 tsp. garlic, chopped

2 tsp. shallots, chopped

½ tsp. kosher salt

¼ tsp. white pepper

¼ lb. cream cheese

¼ wheel Boursin cheese

½ cup mozzarella, shredded

¼ cup Parmesan cheese, shredded

¼ cup heavy cream

½ tsp. Worcestershire sauce

2 Tbsp. Dijon mustard

Serves 6

 MORE DIFFICULT

Combine artichoke hearts, olive oil, white wine, basil, thyme, garlic, shallots, salt and pepper in a baking pan. Roast in a 350-degree oven until brown. Mix cheeses, cream, Worcestershire and mustard in a standing mixer with a paddle until mixed well. Add artichoke mixture to cheese mixture for 2 minutes. Place the incorporated mixture into an oven safe dish, sprinkle with additional mozzarella cheese and bake in a 350-degree oven until golden brown.

SERVING SUGGESTION:
Serve the dip with fresh bread or crostini.

TRUFFLED DEVILED EGGS

MANGY MOOSE RESTAURANT AND SALOON • JACKSON, WYOMING

The Mangy Moose Restaurant and Saloon showcases the best of Jackson Hole with an eclectic vibe, reasonable prices and locally sourced, seasonally fresh food. Since 1967, the Mangy Moose continues to be a must stop in Jackson Hole. Visitors can also explore the Native American jewelry and Mangy Moose gift shops for a Jackson Hole keepsake or gift.

12 eggs, hard-boiled, cooled and shelled

1 Tbsp. Dijon mustard

⅓ cup mayonnaise

¼ tsp. mustard powder

1 tsp. truffle oil

¼ tsp. salt

¼ tsp. white pepper

SERVES 6

EASIEST

Split eggs and remove yolks carefully, then place halved egg whites aside with the yolk cavity facing up. Place yolks in bowl, add all measured ingredients and mix well. With a pastry bag, fill egg whites with yolk mixture.

SERVING SUGGESTION:
Before devouring, drizzle the top of the deviled eggs with truffle oil and sprinkle with paprika.

SERVING SUGGESTION:
Enjoy a refreshing, palette-pleasing High Fashion cocktail, HANDCRAFTED COCKTAIL section,
with this rich après dish.

64   SKI TOWN APRÈS SKI

DUCK CONFIT POUTINE

PLUMPJACK CAFÉ • CHEF BEN "WYATT" DUFRESNE • OLYMPIC VALLEY, CALIFORNIA

Regarded as one of Lake Tahoe's premier dining destinations, PlumpJack Café offers fine dining under the exceptional guidance of Chef Wyatt Dufresne. Changing, seasonal menus take advantage of the bounty of fresh, local produce.

4 - 6 duck legs

4 - 6 Kennebec potatoes, sliced in French fry fashion

Garlic, minced

Fines herbes

Salt and pepper to taste

Cheddar cheese curds, diced

Herb Salt

Green Peppercorn Gravy

SERVES 8 - 10

MOST DIFFICULT

Rub 1 Tbsp. Herb Salt over each leg, rubbing a little extra on the thicker parts and around the joint. Put the legs (flesh side up) in a single layer in a baking dish, cover with plastic wrap and refrigerate for 24 hours.

Preheat oven to 190 degrees. Rinse the legs under cold water and pat dry. Layer the legs (no more than 2 deep) in an ovenproof pot with a lid. Pour melted duck fat over the legs until completely covered. Cook for 8 - 10 hours or until the meat is meltingly tender. Remove the legs from fat and cool on a rack. When cool, remove skin and bones and shred the meat.

Fry potatoes at 350 degrees. Season fries with garlic, fines herbes, salt and pepper. Place the fries in a baking dish and sprinkle with shredded duck confit. Ladle 6 oz. Green Peppercorn Gravy over the top and sprinkle cheese curds over the top. Bake the dish at 500 degrees for 3 - 4 minutes.

HERB SALT

½ cup kosher salt

2 Tbsp. light brown sugar

2 bay leaves, broken into pieces

2 Tbsp. thyme, chopped

¼ cup packed flat-leaf parsley

1 tsp. black peppercorn

Combine all ingredients in a food processor and process until well combined.

GREEN PEPPERCORN GRAVY

1 lb. rice flour

1 lb. unsalted butter

1 gallon heavy cream

1 gallon chicken stock

½ jar green peppercorns, with juice

Kosher salt to taste

Ground black pepper to taste

Melt butter in a pot and whisk in flour. Cook, stirring frequently until roux is well browned. Cool. Bring cream, chicken stock and peppercorns up to boil in a large pot. Whisk in roux until well incorporated. Adjust consistency with chicken stock, if too thick. Season with salt and pepper.

GREEN CHILI & WHITE CHEDDAR MAC & CHEESE

LYNN BRITT CABIN • SNOWMASS, COLORADO

The log cabin was built on historic homestead lands, and its ties to the rustic American West are evident in Lynn Britt Cabin's cuisine — with dishes like Duck Confit Risotto, Bison Meatloaf and the Crispy Skin Chicken served with this recipe. The rich flavors are the result of top-quality, locally harvested ingredients, which come to life through refined cooking techniques.

2 cups heavy cream

1 Poblano pepper

2 Anaheim peppers

2 Tbsp. Spanish onion, diced

4 peppercorns

1 bay leaf

1 garlic clove

1 thyme sprig

8 oz. dried pasta of your choice (Campanelle or Gemelli pasta are recommended)

½ cup Gruyere cheese, shredded

⅔ cup white Vermont cheddar cheese, shredded

1 tsp. olive oil

Salt and pepper to taste

SERVES 4

SERVING SUGGESTION:
Enjoy the richness of this dish, naturally and unadorned.

Preheat oven to broil. Drizzle olive oil over peppers and rub to coat evenly. Place peppers on baking sheet and put under broiler. Cook peppers on each side until the skin is blistered and black. Place peppers in a small bowl and cover tightly with plastic wrap. Allow peppers to rest for 15 minutes, then gently rub the peppers with a paper towel to remove the charred skin. Remove veins and seeds from the peppers and dice.

Place heavy cream, onions, peppercorns, bay leaf, garlic clove and thyme sprig into a saucepot and allow to reduce by a third without coming to a boil. Strain cream and return to sauce pot. While cream is reducing, cook pasta in salted water. Cook pasta a little under al dente and drain; the pasta will be cooked further in the cream sauce.

Add diced peppers to the reduced cream and bring to a simmer. Add pasta to cream sauce and reduce cream by a third. Turn heat to low and slowly add cheese until it is all incorporated and has a silky texture. Turn off heat and season with salt and pepper.

FOCACCIA BREAD

EATS OF EDEN • CHEF TANYA MCFARLAND • EDEN, UTAH

Eats of Eden is located in the ski-centric valley of Eden, Utah. "Eats," as its locally referred, is on the doorstep of Powder Mountain Resort and extremely close to Wolf Mountain Resort, as well. Crowded with skiers and winter-lovers, Eats of Eden serves a wide assortment of delicious comfort food.

4 Tbsp. yeast

2 ½ Tbsp. sugar

2 ½ cups warm water (90—110 degrees)

1 ½ tsp. salt

2 ½ Tbsp. vegetable oil

7 cups all purpose flour, some extra for rolling-out dough

½ cup olive oil

Fresh basil, chopped

3 tomatoes, diced or sliced thin

1 ½ cups mozzarella cheese

Granulated garlic

SERVES 8—10

MORE DIFFICULT

In a mixer, add yeast and sugar. Add warm water to yeast and sugar and let sit for 5 minutes. Add salt, vegetable oil and flour, then mix on low until ingredients come together. Dough should be soft but not stick to fingers. If dough is sticky, add flour by the Tbsp. until it doesn't stick to hands. Water can be added if dough is too tough. Mix until smooth. Turn dough out onto lightly floured surface. Divide evenly into six pieces, as this recipe makes six 9 - 10 oz. focaccia. Knead each section into oval shape and set aside.

Prepare cookie sheet with a light cooking spray. Roll out each section of dough into 4 x 12-inch ovals, place on sheet pan. Two focaccia will fit on one sheet pan. Brush rolled out dough with olive oil. Sprinkle with granulated garlic and basil. Let rest for 10 - 15 minutes. Top with tomatoes and mozzarella cheese. Bake in oven at 450 degrees for 8 minutes or until golden brown. Remove from pan and cut into 8 wedges. Note: Other vegetables, cheeses or meat toppings can be added.

SERVING SUGGESTION:
Serve with your favorite marinara sauce, Alfredo sauce or olive oil and balsamic vinegar. Also, the Italian Cream Soda, HANDCRAFTED COCKTAIL section, compliments the focaccia perfectly.

TRADITIONAL CHEESE FONDUE

CLOUD NINE ALPINE BISTRO • ASPEN, COLORADO

Cloud Nine Alpine Bistro is a legendary Aspen Highlands restaurant that channels authentic European Alpine culture in a warm, welcoming environment. With views of the iconic Maroon Bells - perhaps the American West's most recognizable, postcard-perfect mountains - dining in this cozy, European-style cabin in the Rocky Mountains is a bucket-list worthy experience. What is more European-inspired than a warm and bubbly serving of fondue?!

½ lb. imported Swiss cheese, shredded
(Emmental is recommended)

½ lb. Gruyere cheese, shredded

2 Tbsp. cornstarch

1 fresh garlic clove, peeled

1 cup dry white wine

1 Tbsp. lemon juice

Pinch freshly grated nutmeg

S ERVES **4 - 6**

In a small bowl, coat the cheeses with cornstarch and set aside. Smash the garlic clove then rub the inside of the ceramic fondue pot with the garlic; leave clove in the pot. Over medium heat, add wine and lemon juice and bring to a gentle simmer. Gradually stir the cheese into the simmering liquid. Melting the cheese gradually encourages a smooth fondue. Once smooth, stir in the mustard and nutmeg.

On a platter, arrange an assortment of bite-sized dipping foods around the fondue pot such as Granny Smith apples, French bread, cured salami, pickled vegetables, cornichons and/or sautéed mushrooms.

SERVING SUGGESTION:
The fondue experience is enhanced by sharing with close friends and family.

SERVING SUGGESTION:
Relish the flatbread wedges with a glass of White Sangria,
HANDCRAFTED COCKTAIL section.

ROCKER FLATBREAD

ROCKER@SQUAW • CHEF DANNY MCCABE • OLYMPIC VALLEY, CALIFORNIA

Rocker@Squaw is Squaw Valley's newest restaurant and is a tribute to the many ski legends to come out of the resort over the decades. While much of the menu offers hearty comfort food and gastronomic legends like the 4 lb. G.N.A.R Burger, Rocker has partnered with the Tahoe Food Hub to provide locally and sustainably sourced vegetables—from which the Rocker Flatbread was born.

6 oz. flatbread dough, homemade or locally sourced

1 cup fresh arugula

2 Tbsp. sweet salad dressing (balsamic vinaigrette is recommended)

4 - 5 large Oyster mushrooms, or your choice

Salt and pepper to taste

Herbed Goat Cheese

Pickled Onions

Serves 2 - 4

 MORE DIFFICULT

Slice mushrooms into bite size pieces. Toss with your favorite oil (not olive oil), salt and pepper. Grill or roast mushrooms until done. If you are making dough from scratch, then cook as needed. Once you are ready to build the flatbread, evenly spread the Herbed Goat Cheese on the cooked flatbread. Add grilled mushrooms and bake in the oven at 350 degrees until flatbread is crispy. In the meantime, toss the arugula, Pickled Onions and dressing together with a pinch of salt and pepper. Take the flatbread out of the oven and cut into 8 pieces. Add salad on top.

HERBED GOAT CHEESE

2 oz. goat cheese, room temperature

1 Tbsp. thyme

1 Tbsp. oregano

1 Tbsp. marjoram

Mix thyme, marjoram and oregano into goat cheese. Refrigerate.

PICKLED ONIONS

½ sweet onion, julienned

1 small red beet, trimmed, peeled and cut into 8 pieces

1 garlic clove, peeled and cut into 4 pieces

1 tsp. fennel seed, toasted in sauté pan until seeds are fragrant

2 cups sherry vinegar

⅔ cup sugar

1 bay leaf

Combine sugar, vinegar, beet, bay leaf and toasted fennel in a sauce pot and whisk for a moment. Adjust to high heat and let the liquid come to a boil. Add onions and cook for 3 minutes, remove from heat. Place a plate on top of the onions to submerge the onions in the liquid. Let the mixture cool down. Place into new container and refrigerate until chilled. Remove onions from mixture and set both onions and liquid aside.

Cook down the strained vinegar mixture until thick. This can be used with the arugula salad or another meal.

PORTABELLA FRIES

THE TERRACE AT HIGH CAMP • CHEF CHRIS PATRICK • OLYMPIC VALLEY, CALIFORNIA

The Terrace is located at High Camp at Squaw Valley. To get to the restaurant, diners ride Squaw's aerial tram up to elevation 8,200 feet, where the Terrace's floor to ceiling windows offer panoramic views of Lake Tahoe and the Sierra Nevada Mountains.

4 Portabella mushrooms, cut into 4 - 5 strips

2 Tbsp. tempura batter mix

4 Tbsp. water

½ cup all purpose flour

1 cup oil (canola and olive blend is recommended)

½ cup Chipotle Aioli

SERVES **4**

 Put flour in bowl. In another bowl, combine tempura flour and water. Pour about ½-inch of oil in sauté pan and heat over high until hot. Roll mushroom strip in flour, completely coat. Dip into tempura batter then drag strip into oil and release. Cook 20 - 30 seconds on each side. Cook 3 - 4 at a time. Remove and place on paper towel and drain. Repeat with remaining mushroom strips. Place 2 - 3 Tbsp. of Chipotle Aioli in a martini glass and fill with portabella fries.

CHIPOTLE AIOLI

1 cup mayonnaise

1 chipotle in adobo sauce

1 Tbsp. Sriracha

Splash red wine vinegar

2 Tbsp. fresh lime juice

Salt and pepper to taste

Blend all ingredients together.

SERVING SUGGESTION:
Prior to placing fries in the martini glass, toss with grated Parmesan cheese, chili flakes and chopped parsley. Enjoy the fries with a Hot Apple Pie cocktail, HANDCRAFTED COCKTAIL section.

ARANCINI
with Vialone Nano, Porcini Mushrooms, Boschetto al Tartufo

LEONORA AT THE SEBASTIAN HOTEL • VAIL, COLORADO

Leonora, located at The Sebastian Hotel, debuted with an energetic and warm ambiance and cuisine inspired by the Alps, Pyrenees and local Rocky Mountains. Leonora utilizes only the finest fresh, local and organic ingredients to create tantalizing tapas, crudo and Alpine bistro fare. Leonora's recipes call for simply prepared and flavorful dishes, like the Arancini.

Mushroom Risotto, cooked and seasoned

Boschetto al Tartufo, medium dice

Flour

Truffle Aioli

S ERVES **12**

Use golf ball size of Mushroom Risotto and stuff with diced Boschetto al Tartufo cheese. Roll into an even ball and roll it in flour while it is still lukewarm and moist. Heat oil for frying in a deep saucepan to 350 degrees. Fry the balls in small batches until evenly golden, turning as needed. Drain on paper towels. Keep warm in a low oven while the rest are frying. You can freeze prepared balls and reheat in an oven at 350 degrees for 25 minutes.

MUSHROOM RISOTTO

2 Tbsp. extra virgin olive oil

¼ yellow onion, finely chopped

3 cups Vialone Nano rice

½ cup pinot grigio, room temperature

½ gallon Mushroom Broth, seasoned and hot (you can substitute vegetable broth)

Using a wide pot, sweat onions in olive oil for two minutes at low temperature. Add the rice and continue sweating. Stir constantly until the rice becomes translucent at the edges, but still white in the center. Add wine and let it reduce at very low temperature, so rice absorbs liquid. Cook until most of the liquid has evaporated (au sec).

Add 1 cup Mushroom Broth and stir continuously until almost all the liquid has evaporated. Repeat the process and stir gently at all times until rice is cooked through. Vegetable broth can be substituted for ease. Season risotto when done.

Prepare a sheet pan lined with parchment paper and pour the rice on top. Spread it in an even layer and cool down immediately.

SERVING SUGGESTION:
Enjoy the Arancini drizzled with Truffle Aioli.

MUSHROOM BROTH

2 quarts vegetable broth

12 cups porcini mushrooms, dried

1 yellow onion, halved and grilled

1 sprig fresh thyme

1 bay leaf

Kosher salt to taste

Black pepper to taste, freshly cracked

Mix the ingredients in a stockpot and bring to a boil. Simmer for 25 - 30 minutes.

Taste, adjust seasoning and use to cook the risotto.

TRUFFLE AIOLI

2 whole eggs

1 lemon, juiced and zested

2 Tbsp. Dijon mustard

3 garlic cloves

Kosher salt to taste

Black pepper to taste

White truffle oil and blended oil

Mix ingredients in a blender and purée until smooth. Drizzle oil on top while blender is still running to create an emulsion. Add ice water to adjust the consistency if needed. Taste and adjust seasoning. Put the aioli into two different plastic pastry bags.

ROASTED CAULIFLOWER

COLORFUL COOKING • CHEF TRACY MILLER • VAIL VALLEY, COLORADO

Colorful Cooking's mission is to add a pinch of color to every meal with fruits and vegetables. Colorful Cooking cuisine incorporates simple instruction with a variety of foods to make a body stronger by achieving the recommended five cups of daily fruits and vegetables.

1 head cauliflower

2 Tbsp. olive oil

2 - 3 tsp. kosher salt

2 tsp. dried parsley

1 Tbsp. capers (optional)

S ERVES 4

Heat oven to 425 degrees. Cut cauliflower into ¾-inch pieces by using a large knife and slicing down the center (exposing the core), then removing the core and leaves. Slice each half (like bread) into 3 pieces, then cut each piece into smaller pieces. Rinse cauliflower and drain with paper towels.

Incorporate olive oil, 2 tsp. salt and parsley in a large bowl. Chop and mix in capers, if using. Add cauliflower to olive oil mixture and toss with hands. Arrange mixture in a single layer on a baking sheet and roast for 20 minutes. Remove and stir to a single layer, add salt to taste and roast for 15 minutes until browned.

SERVING SUGGESTION:
Enjoy hot or room temperature, as a side dish or starter.

WHITE BEAN MASH

COLORFUL COOKING • CHEF TRACY MILLER • VAIL VALLEY, COLORADO

The White Bean Mash spread is extremely healthful, as beans and mushrooms are high in protein, folate and fiber. Additionally, mushrooms are considered one of the most medicinal and cancer-fighting foods.

14 oz. can northern white beans, rinsed and drained

1 Tbsp. butter

3 garlic cloves, roasted

1 tsp. truffle oil

½ tsp. kosher salt

2 tsp. white wine vinegar

2 Tbsp. water

1 cup mushrooms, sliced

SERVES 4 - 6

EASIEST

To roast garlic, cut off top of garlic head, pour olive oil over the cut side, wrap in aluminum foil and bake at 400 degrees for 50 minutes, until dark brown and soft.

Heat beans and butter up in a saucepan. Transfer to a blender and add next five ingredients; blend well. Add more water for creamier texture. Keep warm over low on stovetop.

SERVING SUGGESTION:
Serve this with sliced, raw mushrooms and crackers. The White Bean Mash also pairs very well with lamb.

PAN FRIED SQUASH & CRAB PUDDING

LAUNDRY KITCHEN AND COCKTAILS • CHEF ERIC LASLOW • STEAMBOAT SPRINGS, COLORADO

A long running signature dish of Chef Eric Laslow's, Pan Fried Squash and Crab Pudding won the "People's Choice Award" at a Crab Cake Cook Off and landed Chef Laslow on network morning shows, in the Oregonian *newspaper and in regional magazines. He went on to open Laslow's Northwest, which earned the distinction of "Best Restaurants in America" in* Gourmet Magazine *as well as "Restaurant of the Year" from the* Oregonian. *Chef Eric continues his success with Laundry Kitchen and Cocktails, where he continually reflects on this life-changing recipe.*

1 lb. crab, picked for cartilage

2 egg yolks

5 eggs

½ tsp. red curry paste

¾ cup whipping cream

½ cup butternut squash, roasted and pureed

2 Tbsp. chives, chopped

½ tsp. salt (or, to taste)

Panko (Japanese style bread crumbs)

3 Tbsp. canola oil

Pepita Vinaigrette

Fennel Apple Slaw

SERVES 6

MOST DIFFICULT

Preheat oven to 350 degrees. Halve a squash lengthwise and remove seeds. Brush the flesh sides with oil. Sprinkle with salt and pepper. Place face down on an oiled cookie sheet, bake until fork tender. Remove from oven, cool and puree in food processor. Then, add four eggs to help make the mixture smooth.

In a small saucepan, heat 2 Tbsp. cream, add curry paste and dissolve paste in cream until smooth. In a large bowl, combine egg yolks, remaining cream, chives, curry mixture and squash mixture. Whip to a creamy consistency.

Place crab in a colander. Drain any excess moisture and pick through to remove any cartilage. Add crab to egg/squash mixture. Season with salt.

Line a 2-inch baking or casserole dish with six 4 oz. ramekins, which have been rubbed with oil. Fill ramekins with mixture. Move to oven and carefully pour water into dish holding ramekins - water should reach 2/3 up sides of ramekins. Cover loosely with foil and bake for 50 minutes. Remove ramekins from water pan and cool to room temperature. Run a sharp knife around sides and tap out onto a cool surface.

In a small bowl, whip remaining egg with 1 Tbsp. water. In a separate bowl, pour in bread crumbs. Lightly press the top and bottom of each "cake" into the egg wash and then lightly press into panko. Chill. Then, in remaining canola oil, sauté crab pudding in a large pan over medium-high heat on both sides until golden brown. Drizzle Pepita Vinaigrette over plate. Place Fennel Apple Slaw over vinaigrette and top with Crab Pudding.

SERVING SUGGESTION:
Enjoy with Laundry's Cocktail #18, HANDCRAFTED COCKTAIL section, which draws on the combination of acid and earthiness to embrace the richness of the crab pudding.

PEPITA VINAIGRETTE

2 Tbsp. garlic, chopped

2 Tbsp. shallot, chopped

¼ cup pepitas (pumpkin seeds)

2 Tbsp. parsley, chopped

2 Tbsp. chives, chopped

3 Tbsp. rice vinegar

3 Tbsp. champagne vinegar

1 Tbsp. lime juice

7 ½ cups extra virgin olive oil

1 Tbsp. green chili powder

1 ½ Tbsp. green chilies, roasted and chopped

Salt and pepper to taste

In sauté pan, cook garlic and shallot in half the oil. Add pepitas over low heat and sauté until golden. Remove from heat, strain and reserve oil. Let cool to room temperature. Combine with chopped chilies, vinegars and lime in blender. While blending, add chives and parsley. Slowly add oil and emulsify. Season with salt, pepper and chili powder after emulsification. Chill.

FENNEL APPLE SLAW

½ cup fennel, finely shaved

¼ cup red onion, finely shaved

½ cup green apple, finely shaved

2 Tbsp. fresno chilies, finely shaved

¼ cup extra virgin olive oil

1 Tbsp. sherry vinegar

¼ tsp. truffle salt

½ cup Italian parsley leaves, whole

Combine all ingredients in a mixing bowl, toss and chill.

JALAPENO POPPERS

SIDEWINDER SALOON AT MONARCH MOUNTAIN • MONARCH, COLORADO

The Sidewinder Restaurant and Saloon offers a great southwest inspired menu and sit down service, while The Gunbarrel Cafeteria has all the ski-day favorites: burgers, pizza, chili, soups, a salad bar and beverages. There is also Pioneer Room, Elmo's Bar and Java Stop. Enough food outlets to keep skiers fed and fueled for their day of exploring Monarch Mountain's varied terrain.

1 cup cream cheese, softened

½ cup Monterey jack and cheddar blend, finely shredded

¼ cup corn, fire-roasted

1 Tbsp. ground cumin

Salt and pepper to taste

Bacon, thickly sliced

12 fresh jalapenos

SERVES 6

Combine all ingredients except bacon and jalapenos for the filling. Mix with a wooden spoon. Cut the tops off the jalapenos and remove seeds with a corer. Using a teaspoon, stuff poppers with filling (a pastry bag works well to pipe the filling into the jalapenos as long as the filling is softened). Take one piece of bacon and place over the top of the jalapeno to cover the filling. Wrap the rest of the bacon around the sides of the jalapeno. Push a toothpick through the end of the bacon all the way through the jalapeno to hold the bacon in place. Roast the bacon-wrapped stuffed jalapenos at 425 degrees for 20 minutes until the bacon is cooked and cheese is melted. Serve immediately.

SERVING SUGGESTION:
Enjoy these spicy treats with the pictured Bloody Mary, HANDCRAFTED COCKTAIL section.

LOVELAND SKI AREA HUMMUS

LOVELAND SKI AREA • GEORGETOWN, COLORADO

Covered with an average of 400 inches of snow per year, Loveland Ski Area offers skiing for all types. With the variety of eating options at Loveland, foodies will find hearty sandwiches, Mexican food, savory pastas, homemade soups, made-to-order pizzas and an outdoor barbecue on the Basin deck.

5 cups garbanzo beans

4 Tbsp. tahini

2 lemons, juiced and zested

¼ cup garlic, roasted

¼ cup olive oil

2 tsp. cumin

Salt and pepper to taste

SERVES 8

Put all ingredients, except oil, into food processor and mix well. Fresh garlic can be used in place of roasted garlic, but roasted garlic gives a smoother texture and adds a deeper flavor. Slowly add olive oil during mixing. Add salt and pepper to taste.

SERVING SUGGESTION:
Enjoy this dip with crackers and vegetables of your choice.

FOUNDRY GRILL PROSCIUTTO PIZZA

FOUNDRY GRILL • PROVO, UTAH

The Foundry Grill, of which the name implies simplicity and a return to the fundamentals, captures the essence of this definition in its room, the service, and the menu. The Foundry Grill is committed to providing the freshest of vegetables and meats cooked to order. In warm weather, the patio opens for outside dining. As Sundance believes in the preservation of our resources, all table centerpieces are created from recycled glass hand blown at Sundance Resort.

Pizza dough

Sliced prosciutto

Rapine with leaves

Rosemary Tomato Jam

Pickled red onions

Timpanogos Peak Blue Cheese

Arugula

Rosemary

Thyme

Olive oil

Fleur de Sel

SERVES DESIRED PARTY SIZE

 MORE DIFFICULT

Roll out your choice of pizza dough, spread Rosemary Tomato Jam atop then add your desired amounts of prosciutto, rapine, onions and blue cheese. Brush the pizza crust with olive oil infused with rosemary, thyme and garlic. Finish with fleur de sel. Bake at dough recommended temperature, until cheese is melted and crust is golden. (You can prebake the crust to ensure crispiness.)

ROSEMARY TOMATO JAM

4 whole heirloom tomatoes, diced

Sweet garlic, diced

Shallots, diced

Olive oil

Pectin

Fresh thyme

Banjul's vinegar

Sugar

Mix tomatoes, garlic and shallots together with a little olive oil. To a medium-high heat saucepan on the stovetop, add tomato mixture 1 cup at a time with pectin until pectin develops and thickens. Bring to rolling boil, stirring. Add fresh thyme and Banjul's vinegar. Also, add sugar if needed. Pass through a colander.

SERVING SUGGESTION:
Top with a handful of vibrant arugula.

LOBSTER NACHOS

SILVER DOLLAR BAR AND GRILL • CHEF WILLIAM PEAK • JACKSON, WYOMING

Located inside the historic Wort Hotel, just off the town square in downtown Jackson, the elegant Silver Dollar Bar and Grill offers a memorable Western dining experience. Custom black-walnut tables, doors and millwork showcase even finer details in stained glass and over three hundred 1921 Morgan Silver Dollars inlaid throughout. The interior highlights original western artwork, a restored original Wort Hotel roulette wheel and deliciously prepared game and regional fare.

⅜ cup lobster

¼ cup chorizo

¼ cup black beans, cooked

¼ cup Avocado Relish

2 Tbsp. spicy sour cream

Sriracha to taste

¼ cup Cotija cheese, grated

2 blue corn tortillas, medium-sized and halved

3 sprigs of cilantro

Small amount butter

Vegetable oil

SERVES 2

Preheat oven to 450 degrees. In a skillet, brown chorizo until fully cooked, discard grease. In a separate saucepan, heat butter to a small boil and add chopped lobster. Slowly boil for 5 minutes and drain butter. Heat vegetable oil over medium-high heat, cook tortillas in oil until crisp, about 4 - 5 minutes. Place tortillas on a sheet pan. Mix together sour cream and Sriracha, if you desire spicy sour cream.

In layers on the chips, add chorizo, lobster, black beans and cheese. Heat for 5 minutes and take out of oven. Top with Avocado Relish and sour cream.

Garnish with cilantro.

AVOCADO RELISH

1 avocado

Lime wedge

1 Tbsp. tomato, seeded and small diced

1 Tbsp. onion, small diced

1 Tbsp. red pepper, small diced

1 tsp. cilantro, chopped

Salt to taste

Scoop out inside of avocado in small bowl. Add the juice of lime, tomatoes, onions, red peppers and cilantro. Season with salt. Mix all ingredients together and set aside.

SERVING SUGGESTION:

The Lobster Nachos are spectacular with the Bartender's Margarita, HANDCRAFTED COCKTAIL section.

BUFFALO GORGONZOLA MEATBALLS
in Orange Sweet Chili Sauce

JIMMY B'S AT BRIDGER BOWL • BOZEMAN, MONTANA

On the 2nd floor of the Jim Bridger Lodge, Jimmy B's has a full pub-style menu with table service, full-service bar featuring local and regional microbrews, a wood-burning fireplace and live music on weekends and holidays. The ski area offers a nice transitional progression from a first-time beginner slope in the base area to novice terrain across the lower middle, wide-open intermediate runs in the center, advanced open bowl terrain in the upper third and, finally, expert terrain coming off the ridge top.

1 lb. bison, ground

½ cup bread crumbs

1 cup gorgonzola cheese, crumbled

½ small onion, finely diced

3 garlic cloves, minced

½ tsp. Worcestershire sauce

1 tsp. salt

½ tsp. black pepper

½ tsp. basil

Orange Sweet Chili Sauce

SERVES **4**

Preheat oven to 400 degrees. Mix together all ingredients; be careful not to over mix. Lightly roll the mixture into 2-inch meatballs and place them on sheet pans. Brush meatballs with olive oil; this will brown them nicely. Bake for 35 - 40 minutes, until the tops are browned and the centers are completely cooked. You can pan fry these meatballs in a little oil on the stovetop as well. Once the meatballs are cooked, cover them with Orange Sweet Chili Sauce and arrange on a platter.

ORANGE SWEET CHILI SAUCE

2 large seedless oranges, juiced

1 lemon, juiced

3 cups water

1 cup rice vinegar or white vinegar

3 cups sugar

2 tsp. fresh ginger root, minced

1 tsp. garlic, minced

2 tsp. hot chili pepper, minced

2 tsp. ketchup

2 tsp. cornstarch

Mix together all ingredients. Boil to dissolve sugar. Set aside.

SERVING SUGGESTION:
Enjoy the meatballs with a Loco Kokoa cocktail, HANDCRAFTED COCKTAIL section.

SEA & SURF

SHRIMP AND GRITS

CHEF KELLY LIKEN • VAIL, COLORADO

Chef Kelly Liken is known for offering simple, yet exciting Seasonal American Cuisine that relies heavily on locally produced and cultivated products.

20 large shrimp, peeled and deveined

4 Tbsp. butter

1 Tbsp. shallots, minced

1 lemon, juiced

4 Tbsp. parsley, chopped

Tomato Lobster Sauce

Grits

SERVES 4

MORE DIFFICULT

Preheat a sauté pan on medium high heat and melt butter. Then, add shrimp. Sauté 2 - 3 minutes on one side, or until shrimp are pink. Flip shrimp and finish cooking. Once shrimp are mostly cooked, add shallots, lemon juice and parsley.

In the center of 4 plates, make a small mound of Grits. Neatly spoon the Tomato Lobster Sauce around the ring. Place 5 shrimp on top of Grits and dress with the shallot-lemon-butter sauce from the sauté pan.

SERVING SUGGESTION:
Enjoy this dish with a lovely handcrafted cocktail from Kelly Liken.

TOMATO LOBSTER SAUCE

½ red onion, julienned

¼ cup bacon, brunoised

¼ jalapeno, brunoised

½ roasted red pepper, julienned

Pinch crushed red pepper flakes

Pinch cayenne pepper

Pinch cumin

⅛ tsp. salt

⅛ tsp. black pepper

Sachet of 4 thyme sprigs and ½ bay leaf

2 cups lobster stock

1 cup tomato juice

Render bacon until crispy, strain and reserve fat. Pour ¾ of bacon fat back into the pan and sweat onions and jalapeños until soft. Add roasted red peppers, dry spices, salt and pepper. Then, add lobster stock and tomato juice. Simmer and cook on low for 20 minutes.

GRITS

1 Tbsp. shallots, brunoised

½ cup grits

1 cup chicken stock

½ cup butter

Salt and pepper to taste

Sweat shallots in a small amount of butter until translucent. Add chicken stock and bring to a boil with salt and pepper. When liquid comes to a boil, add a little more butter. Slowly whisk in grits. Cook grits on medium high heat until they start to thicken. Whisk constantly, ensuring grits have no lumps. When grits are fully cooked and softened, add remaining butter to finish. Adjust seasoning with salt and pepper.

BEER BATTERED FRIED FISH

MAD RIVER GLEN • CHEF MICHAEL WITZEL • WAITSFIELD, VERMONT

General Stark's Pub offers a full bar, hearty pub menu and table service for lunch and après ski. There is often live music in the pub after skiing, a TV for watching sports and a comfortable place to swap ski stories with friends. On the mountain, Birdcage Lodge is open on weekends and holidays offering a menu of grilled sandwiches, hot dogs and sausages, baked goods and a wide variety of hot and cold beverages.

Haddock fillets or another semi-firm white fish

Peanut or canola oil

7 cups all purpose flour

1 ½ Tbsp. kosher salt

1 tsp. cayenne pepper

2 Tbsp. garlic powder

2 Tbsp. onion powder

2 tsp. baking soda

32 oz. Long Trail Ale

SERVES A LARGE PARTY SIZE

MORE DIFFICULT

Whip all ingredients together, except fish fillets and oil. Make sure to remove lumps. The consistency will resemble a pancake batter. Taste and adjust seasoning with salt and cayenne pepper. Let batter rest.

Heat a pot of peanut or canola oil to 350 degrees. Cut fillets to 3 – 4 oz. each. Dip into batter, then holding one end with tongs, add to hot oil. Cook until golden brown on both sides. Drain on paper towels.

SERVING SUGGESTION:
Serve fish with lemon wedge, Tartar Sauce, Clear Coleslaw and a simply fresh Stark & Stormy cocktail, HANDCRAFTED COCKTAIL section.

TARTAR SAUCE

½ gallon mayonnaise

½ cup dill pickle juice

1 dozen pickle spears, minced

¼ cup lemon juice

½ Tbsp. dill

1 Tbsp. capers

¼ Tbsp. chipotle pepper, pureed

Salt and pepper to taste

Mix together; rest, so flavor develops. Adjust seasoning.

CLEAR COLESLAW

1 head green cabbage, julienned

2 red onions, julienned

2 Tbsp. cilantro, chopped

2 cups white vinegar

1 cup lime juice

1 ½ cups sugar

1 ½ Tbsp. kosher salt

2 tsp. dried red pepper flakes

Whip last five ingredients together until sugar and salt dissolve, then toss with first three ingredients. Macerate in the refrigerator for 1 hour or more. Adjust seasoning, if needed.

AHI TUNA TACOS

MT. HOOD MEADOWS • MT. HOOD, OREGON

Mt. Hood Meadows, under the slogan: Nourish - Replenish - Refresh - Enjoy - Be Entertained and Have Fun, offers nine eating establishments at the resort. In between fantastic ski runs, a skier can stop for a refreshing, tasty, delicious and healthful meal. These energy breaks will make for a more enjoyable day.

2 taco shells

1 ½ oz. Ahi tuna, prepared medium rare

1 ½ oz. chipotle coleslaw

Wasabi guacamole

SERVES 1

In your favorite taco shells (soft or hard), add half the tuna per taco with chipotle coleslaw. You can prepare your normal coleslaw recipe and add 1 small canned chipotle chili, minced, a spoonful of adobo sauce from the can and a few chopped cilantro leaves. Top each taco with wasabi guacamole, which can be your normal guacamole recipe with just a bit of wasabi powder.

SERVING SUGGESTION:
Serve these tacos with chips and tomatillo salsa. Also, pair this with a Bloody Mary, HANDCRAFTED COCKTAIL section.

PAN SEARED SEA SCALLOPS

ANDIAMO ITALIAN GRILLE • CHEF TYLER SLOAN • BIG SKY, MONTANA

In Italian, Andiamo translates to "let's go!" Big Sky Resort's restaurant surely approaches this literally, serving everything from salads and appetizers to pasta dishes and steak, with a very Tuscan-flavor profile. Or, "Tuscany with a twist," states Chef Sloan.

3 large scallops

2 Tbsp. extra virgin olive oil

3 scallions, cut on a steep bias

Polenta

Marinated Red Peppers

Crispy Pancetta

SERVES 1

In a sauté pan, add extra virgin olive oil and heat to smoking. Add scallops and cook until nicely seared on each side. Take them out of the pan, then add 1 Tbsp. of Marinated Peppers and turn off heat.

To plate, put ½ cup Polenta on a plate, then top with scallops. Take Marinated Peppers from pan and top each scallop with them. Garnish with Crispy Pancetta and scallions.

POLENTA

1 cup milk

½ cup heavy cream

¼ cup Anson-Mills Polenta

½ cup Parmesan cheese

Small sprig rosemary

Salt and pepper to taste

Scald milk, cream and rosemary in a heavy bottom pot. Slowly whisk in the polenta and bring to a slow simmer, stirring frequently. Simmer until it thickens and loosens the gritty texture. Add Parmesan, salt and pepper.

MARINATED RED PEPPERS

1 red pepper

5 Tbsp. extra virgin olive oil

3 Tbsp. sherry wine vinegar

2 Tbsp. chopped parsley

Salt and pepper to taste

Roast peppers in oven, cool and then peel. Dice peppers into small pieces. In a bowl, add peppers, extra virgin olive oil, sherry vinegar, parsley, salt and pepper and let sit for 3 hours.

CRISPY PANCETTA

¼ cup extra virgin olive oil

½ cup pancetta, chiffonade

Put extra virgin olive oil in a sauté pan and heat on medium. Add pancetta, and keep an eye on it because it will burn easily. Once golden brown, remove from oil and let dry.

SAUTÉED LITTLENECK CLAMS
with Tasso, Roasted Fennel, Spicy Broth and a Grilled Baguette

SKAMANIA LODGE • CHEF MARK HENRY • STEVENSON, WASHINGTON

At Skamania Lodge in Stevenson, Washington, there is a selection of dining experiences to meet every request. The award-winning Cascade Dining Room is a highlight of this Portland-area resort, featuring Pacific Northwest cuisine, the Gorge Harvest Buffet served every Friday night and the Sunday Champagne Brunch. River Rock Restaurant offers lighter fare to be enjoyed by the river rock fireplace. And, dining al fresco may be enjoyed at River Rock or at The Greenside Grille.

16 littleneck clams

1 oz. Tasso ham, julienned

1 oz. fennel, julienned

1 medium shallot, minced

2 garlic cloves, minced

1 Tbsp. fresh jalapeno, finely diced

1 Tbsp. vegetable oil

½ cup clam juice

½ cup V-8 juice

2 oz. Dry Fly Washington wheat bourbon

4 Tbsp. cold butter

Chives, chopped

1 slice baguette, grilled

S ERVES 2

EASIEST

Season fennel with salt and pepper and slightly roast in the oven at 350 degrees for about 4 - 5 minutes. Sauté ham, roasted fennel, garlic, shallots and jalapeno in vegetable oil for 2 - 3 minutes over medium heat. Deglaze the pan with bourbon, flambé for a minute then add the V-8 and clam juice. Let liquid reduce by half, then add the clams and cook in broth until clams open. Add cold butter to thicken broth. Dish into a shallow bowl.

SERVING SUGGESTION:
Add chopped chives to clams and a slice of grilled baguette.
Enjoy this dish with a refreshing Lime-Aid cocktail, HANDCRAFTED COCKTAIL section.

LARKSPUR MUSSELS & CALAMARI

LARKSPUR RESTAURANT • VAIL, COLORADO

Known as one of the best restaurants in Vail for hosting weddings on their event lawn, Larkspur Restaurant is also one of the best après ski locations, as it is at the base of Vail Mountain – Golden Peak location. Larkspur has also been voted as the best large party venue.

1 tsp. parsley, minced

1 tsp. lemon zest, minced

1 tsp. garlic, minced

½ tsp. chili flakes

½ tsp. salt

½ tsp. black pepper, coarsely ground

1 cup extra virgin olive oil

5 oz. calamari, rinsed and cut into ½-inch rings

8 oz. mussels, rinsed under cool water, discard any open mussels

1 cup Gremolata

1 Tbsp. blended oil (80% canola oil and 20% olive oil)

Kosher salt

SERVES 2

 MORE DIFFICULT

In a medium-size bowl, mix parsley, lemon zest, garlic, chili flakes, salt and pepper; slowly add olive oil until mixture becomes a loose sauce. Add calamari and mix until evenly coated. Marinate for 20 minutes.

On stovetop, heat a medium-size, cast-iron skillet to 500 degrees. Cook mussels evenly, until all opened, about 5 minutes. Discard any mussels that do not open. It is very hard to overcook mussels, so do not rush.

In another sauté pan, while mussels are cooking, heat blended oil until it begins to smoke. Cook calamari for 1 minute or until rings begin to turn opaque. Be careful not to over-cook, as calamari will develop a rubbery texture.

When mussels are ready, season with kosher salt and spoon generous amounts of Gremolata over mussels. Pan will sizzle loudly and oil will pop, so be careful not to burn yourself. Pour mussels and juice into a shallow serving bowl, and place calamari on top. Serve hot.

SERVING SUGGESTION:
Relish a taste of the sea with a Mayahuela's Margarita, HANDCRAFTED COCKTAIL section.

GREMOLATA

1 bunch parsley

1 quart blended oil (80% canola and 20% olive)

2 lemons, zested

2 garlic cloves

1 Tbsp. salt

YIELDS 4 CUPS

Place oil in a blender and cool for at least 20 minutes in a freezer. Add garlic and parsley, including stems. Puree on low, gradually increasing speed to high. Puree will begin white and then turn bright green when it is ready. Do not puree too long, as oil may become bitter and heat will cause the parsley to brown. Put puree in a bowl and add lemon zest, whisking to incorporate. Add salt to taste.

8100 POPCORN FISH 'N CHIPS

8100 MOUNTAINSIDE BAR AND GRILL • CHEF CHRISTIAN APETZ • AVON, COLORADO

This vastly changing, seasonal menu invites endless palettes to indulge at 8100. Specializing in local, natural and organic dishes complemented by Colorado's best craft beers, wines and spirits, 8100 is the embodiment of mountain sophistication. At the centerpiece of the open kitchen is the grill, capturing smoke-infused flavors befitting the Colorado Mountains. Guests enjoy outdoor dining and gathering areas around cozy fire pits overlooking the Rockies.

1 lb. firm white fish (snapper), diced into ½-inch cubes

2 cups buttermilk

¼ cup coarse corn meal

¾ cup all-purpose flour

2 Tbsp. Old Bay seasoning

1 Tbsp. salt

Homemade Chips

Tartar Sauce

SERVES 2

Soak white fish cubes in buttermilk for 2 – 12 hours. Mix together corn meal, flour, seasoning and salt. Toss fish in corn meal mixture until fully coated. Fry in vegetable oil at 350 degrees for 5 - 7 minutes or until fully cooked. Drain on paper towels.

HOMEMADE CHIPS

3 russet potatoes, ¹⁄₁₆-inch thick slices

Vegetable oil

3 Tbsp. fresh dill, chopped

1 ½ Tbsp. Old Bay seasoning

Salt to taste

Slice potatoes with a mandolin. Fry in vegetable oil at 300 degrees for 5 - 8 minutes or until golden brown. Mix together dill, seasoning and salt. Remove chips from oil and sprinkle with dill mixture. Drain on paper towels.

TARTAR SAUCE

1 lemon, juiced and zested

1 cup mayonnaise

1 Tbsp. apple cider vinegar

1 tsp. salt

Mix all ingredients vigorously with a spoon until it has uniform consistency.

SERVING SUGGESTION:

Serve fried fish with Homemade Chips and Tartar Sauce. The Ski Breeze cocktail, HANDCRAFTED COCKTAIL section, pairs very well with this dish.

MOJAVE SHRIMP

CHET'S BAR AND GRILL • BIG SKY, MONTANA

Chet's Bar and Grill, located in the Huntley Lodge at Big Sky Resort, serves a variety of mouth-watering sustenance. From a sumptuous breakfast to hearty appetizers, salad and steak for dinner alongside a handcrafted Montana micro-brew, enjoy this celebrated après ski spot.

5 jumbo shrimp

1 jalapeno, seeded and cut into strips

3 slices of bacon, cut in half

Special BBQ Sauce

Corn Salsa

Lemon zest

SERVES 1 - 2

MORE DIFFICULT

Peel and devein shrimp. Place 1 jalapeno strip where the vein was. Wrap in bacon. Skewer 5 shrimp on 1 skewer. Brush with Special BBQ Sauce and place on a hot grill. Turn after 2 - 3 minutes, basting with Special BBQ Sauce. On a plate, spoon Corn Salsa in the center. When shrimp are finished, brush shrimp one more time with Special BBQ Sauce and then remove from skewer onto plate. Drizzle a little more Special BBQ Sauce on shrimp and plate, sprinkle lemon zest on top.

SPECIAL BBQ SAUCE

1 Tbsp. butter

2 shallots, diced

1 Tbsp. black pepper, coarsely ground

1 cup apple cider vinegar

1 cup Coca Cola

2 cups BBQ sauce, your favorite

¼ cup maple syrup

In a small saucepan, heat butter and add shallots. Cook over medium-high heat until shallots begin to brown. Add black pepper and stir in, cooking only for a few more seconds. Add vinegar and Coca Cola and reduce by half. Add BBQ sauce and syrup, bring to a boil and simmer for 5 minutes. For a smoother sauce, strain to remove shallots.

CORN SALSA

1 Tbsp. light olive oil

2 cups corn kernels

¼ cup cilantro, roughly chopped

½ cup red bell pepper, diced

1 Tbsp. lime juice

1 tsp. Cholula hot sauce

1 tsp. kosher salt

1 fresh jalapeno, minced

Heat oil in a sauté pan and add corn. Sauté until corn is slightly browned, about 3 - 5 minutes. Place in a container and cool. Once cooled, incorporate corn with remaining ingredients.

SERVING SUGGESTION:
Serve alongside Northwest special Huckleberry Lemonade, HANDCRAFTED COCKTAIL section.

SMOKED SALMON POTATO PANCAKES

FORMERLY OF BUFFALO GAL • CHEF TOM STEINBERG • DONNELLY, IDAHO

Potato pancakes are shallow-fried pancakes made of grated or ground potato, matza meal or flour and a binding agent such as egg or applesauce. This pancake if flavored with salmon, garlic, onion and hot sauce.

15 oz. frozen hash browns

8 oz. smoked salmon, flaked

1 small red onion, diced

½ leek, julienned

3 eggs

½ cup Italian parsley, chopped

1 Tbsp. granulated garlic

1 Tbsp. onion powder

1 Tbsp. black pepper

1 Tbsp. Frank's RedHot sauce

1 Tbsp. lemon juice

½ cup flour

1 tsp. kosher salt

SERVES 6 – 8

Put eggs in mixing bowl with salt, parsley, garlic powder, onion powder, black pepper, hot sauce and lemon juice; whisk lightly. Add potatoes, onions and leeks; mix to coat. Add salmon and mix lightly. Add flour and mix until incorporated. Form and fry pancakes in melted, clarified butter in a cast iron skillet until golden brown on both sides.

SERVING SUGGESTION:
Serve with chive cream cheese and applesauce.

PAN SEARED SESAME TUNA

LONGFELLOW'S RESTAURANT • CHEF CHRISTOPHER DOUCETTE • KINGFIELD, MAINE

Longfellow's Restaurant has been in Chef Christopher's family for over 30 years and recently, he and his wife took over ownership. Chef Chris continues displaying his passion for cooking by creating delicious food and new menu ideas, including quite a few vegan-centric dishes.

½ cup fresh sashimi-grade Ahi (yellow fin) tuna

Black and white sesame seeds

1 Tbsp. peanut or sesame oil

1 tsp. ginger, pickled

½ tsp. wasabi paste

Lemon wedge

⅛ cup seaweed salad

1 ½ Tbsp. Sweet Asian Soy Sauce

SERVES 1

Heat a medium-sized skillet to high heat with peanut oil until pan starts to smoke, about 1 ½ minutes. Coat tuna with an even mix of black and white sesame seeds and carefully place tuna in skillet using tongs. Flip only once after 3 - 6 seconds depending on thickness and desired temperature. Cooking time should be equal on both sides. After desired temperature is reached, pull from skillet and place on paper towel to absorb any excess oil. Move to cutting board and slice on the bias.

Garnish serving plate with pickled ginger, wasabi, a lemon wedge, seaweed salad and a small ramekin of the Sweet Asian Soy Sauce. Fan out tuna over the seaweed salad.

SWEET ASIAN SOY SAUCE

⅓ cup soy sauce

⅓ cup honey

¼ cup rice vinegar

⅛ cup sherry

¼ tsp. crushed red pepper flakes

2 tsp. ginger root, freshly grated

2 tsp. garlic, freshly minced

Combine all ingredients in a bowl, mix well and chill in refrigerator for about an hour.

SERVING SUGGESTION:
Enjoy this revitalizing appetizer with a High Speed Cocktail, HANDCRAFTED COCKTAIL section.

SEARED DIVER SCALLOPS
with Sautéed Crimini Mushrooms & Fennel, Parmesan & Herb Risotto & Béarnaise Sauce

SALMON RIVER BREWERY • CHEF JASON VANSLYKE • MCCALL, IDAHO

Salmon River Brewery makes craft beer using as many local and regional ingredients as possible. The restaurant and pub is family-friendly with outdoor seating in the summer, featuring live music.

10 fresh U-10 diver scallops

4 Tbsp. olive oil

Salt and pepper to taste

Sautéed Crimini Mushrooms and Fennel

Parmesan and Herb Risotto

Béarnaise Sauce

SERVES 2

 MOST DIFFICULT

Divide oil between two large sauté pans over high heat. Heat oil until almost smoking. Divide seasoned scallops between pans; do not crowd. Cook until dark brown, about 2 minutes. Turn scallops and cook for 1 - 2 minutes.

To assemble, spoon a generous serving of Parmesan and Herb Risotto on a plate. Top with Sautéed Crimini Mushrooms and Fennel and seared scallops. Finally, drizzle Béarnaise Sauce.

BÉARNAISE SAUCE

½ lb. clarified butter

4 shallots, finely chopped

2 Tbsp. fresh tarragon leaves

4 white peppercorns, crushed

¼ cup white wine vinegar

⅓ cup dry white wine

4 large egg yolks

¼ tsp. salt

Pinch cayenne pepper

Melt butter in a medium saucepan over medium heat. Boil shallots, tarragon and peppercorns in vinegar, wine and melted butter until reduced to about ¼ cup. Strain into the top of a double boiler. Whisk in the egg yolks. Place the top over the bottom of the double boiler containing simmering water. Water should not touch the top pot. Whisk until thickened and season with salt and pepper.

SERVING SUGGESTION:
Enjoy this earthy dish with The Nutty AmBro from Salmon River Brewery.

SAUTÉED CRIMINI MUSHROOMS AND FENNEL

1 large fennel bulb, trimmed and thinly sliced

½ lb. crimini mushrooms, thinly sliced

½ Tbsp. shallot, minced

½ Tbsp. garlic, minced

1 Tbsp. olive oil

½ cup white wine

In a sauté pan over medium-high heat, heat oil. Add garlic and shallots; cook until fragrant, about 30 seconds. Add ¼ cup white wine and reduce by half. Add mushrooms and cook for 2 - 3 minutes or until they begin to soften. Add fennel and cook 2 - 3 minutes. Add remaining white wine. Season with salt and pepper to taste.

PARMESAN AND HERB RISOTTO

6 cups chicken broth

4 Tbsp. unsalted butter

1 large onion, finely chopped (about 1 ½ cups)

1 tsp. garlic, minced or pressed through a garlic press

2 cups Arborio rice

1 cup dry white wine

1 cup Parmesan cheese, grated

1 tsp. fresh lemon juice

2 Tbsp. fresh parsley leaves, chopped

2 Tbsp. fresh chives, chopped

Table salt and ground black pepper to taste

Boil some broth and some water in large saucepan over high heat, then gently simmer over medium-low. Heat 2 Tbsp. butter in a large Dutch oven over medium heat, and add onion and ¾ tsp. salt. Cook, stirring frequently, until onion is softened but not browned, 4 - 7 minutes. Add garlic and stir until fragrant, about 30 seconds. Add rice and cook, stirring frequently, until grains are translucent around edges, about 3 minutes. Add wine and cook, stirring constantly, 2 - 3 minutes. Stir 5 cups hot broth into rice; reduce heat to medium-low. Cover and simmer until almost all liquid has been absorbed and rice is al dente, 16 - 19 minutes, stirring twice during cooking.

Add ¾ cup hot broth mixture and stir gently and constantly until risotto becomes creamy, about 3 minutes. Stir in Parmesan. Remove pot from heat, cover and let stand 5 minutes. Stir in remaining 2 Tbsp. butter, lemon juice, parsley and chives; season with salt and pepper to taste. If desired, add up to ½ cup remaining broth to loosen texture of risotto. Serve immediately.

TROUT CAKES

ENDO'S ADRENALINE BAR AND GRILL • CHEF PHIL BRADY • COPPER MOUNTAIN, COLORADO

A perfect place for après ski, Endo's Adrenaline Bar and Grill has a plethora of appetizers to enjoy: Endo's Mondo nachos, wings, smoked trout dip, shrimp and scallop skewers, as well as this Trout Cakes appetizer.

½ cup raw shrimp, roughly chopped

1 Tbsp. shallots, minced

1 Tbsp. garlic, minced

2 tsp. Old Bay Seasoning

Pinch salt

Pinch pepper

3 Tbsp. mayo

2 large eggs

¾ cup bread crumbs

1 Ruby Red trout fillet, roughly chopped

¼ cup red peppers, minced

2 tsp. fennel, roasted

¼ cup parsley, minced

Butter

SERVES **2-4**

MORE DIFFICULT

Fold all ingredients together, except butter, and portion into 2 oz. patties. Sauté in a cast iron pan at medium heat with a little butter until cakes are pan-seared, golden brown and fully cooked.

SERVING SUGGESTION:
Plate these trout cakes on a bed of spring greens and
top with your choice of aioli.

CRISPY FRIED AVOCADO WITH CRAB

CB (COVERED BRIDGE) GRILLE • CHEF ADAM JESS • COPPER MOUNTAIN, COLORADO

Along with many other enticing appetizers created by Chef Adam Jess, this Crispy Fried Avocado with Crab option is offered on CB Grille's extensive menu. Chef Adam's trademark is blending regional cuisine with world flavors, yet there is nothing pretentious about him or the CB Grille. With fresh local ingredients and a menu that includes a wide range of culinary offerings and specialty drinks, CB Grille is a wonderful place to celebrate the end of the day.

10 oz. Dungeness crab, picked and cleaned

2 Tbsp. red onion, minced

2 Tbsp. cilantro, chopped

2 Tbsp. Anaheim peppers, minced

1 cup Cotija cheese

4 oz. cream cheese, room temperature

1 Tbsp. lime juice

Salt and pepper to taste

2 cups egg wash

2 avocados, halved

Bread crumbs, as needed

¼ cup grilled pineapple, small diced

2 Tbsp. sweet chili sauce

SERVES 4

In a mixer with a paddle attachment, combine crab, onions, peppers, lime and cheeses; season to taste. Slice avocado in half and remove the seed. Slice each half into six slices and fan out on plastic wrap. Measure 2 Tbsp. crab mix and form into a ball. Set crab ball on the middle of the avocado. Pull the plastic wrap up from the sides to form the avocado into a ball surrounding the crab mix. Season the avocado ball with salt and pepper. Dip ball into egg wash and then roll in bread crumbs to coat. Fry in deep fryer at 350 degrees until golden brown. Make a line on a plate with the sweet chili sauce and scatter diced pineapple on top. Set golden balls on plate and serve.

SERVING SUGGESTION:
Just like they do at CB Grille, enjoy the golden treats with grilled pineapple and sweet chili sauce beside a Raspberry Royale Cocktail, HANDCRAFTED COCKTAIL section.

CAMP LOBSTER SLIDERS

CAMP AT GRAND SUMMIT HOTEL • NEWRY, MAINE

The Camp Lobster Sliders are an appetizing indulgence. On toasted yeast rolls, enjoy a lobster salad creatively made with chardonnay, Meyer lemon, tarragon vinaigrette, avocado, lettuce and Backyard Farms tomatoes.

1 lb. Maine lobster, freshly picked, cooked and roughly chopped

1 Tbsp. chardonnay wine

2 Tbsp. fresh Meyer lemon juice or a combination of grapefruit and lemon juice

2 Tbsp. shallot, minced

1 Tbsp. fresh tarragon, chopped

¼ cup celery, small diced

1 Tbsp. Dijon mustard

½ cup mayonnaise

Kosher salt and freshly ground pepper to taste

Yeast rolls

Melted butter

Arugula

Tomatoes, thinly sliced

Avocado, thinly sliced or chopped

SERVES 4 - 6

 MORE DIFFICULT

Mix wine, lemon juice, shallot, tarragon, celery, mustard, mayonnaise, salt and pepper to make a dressing. To the roughly chopped lobster, add dressing until the lobster meat has been coated well.

Toast yeast rolls that have been brushed with melted butter. Spoon a good helping of lobster salad onto the mini yeast rolls (slider buns). Top with baby arugula, thinly sliced tomatoes and avocado.

SERVING SUGGESTION:
A Moonstruck Mule cocktail, HANDCRAFTED COCKTAIL section, is the ultimate pairing for the Lobster Sliders.

SHRIMP BALL SKEWERS
with Sweet Pepper Gastrique & Lime Cream

THE GRILL AT AMANGANI • JACKSON, WYOMING

Amangani, which means a peaceful home, clings to the crest of East Gros Ventre Butte in Jackson Hole. The resort affords magnificent views of the Grand Tetons and Snake River Valley below. As the first Aman resort in North America, Amangani evokes the atmosphere of the American West through all seasons: winter highlights skiing, while in spring, summer and fall, the surrounding wilderness areas of Grand Teton and Yellowstone National Parks are amongst the many attractions.

1 ¼ lbs. shrimp

2 Tbsp. kosher salt

1 Tbsp. smoked sweet paprika (plus an extra pinch for dusting)

2 large shallots, minced

3 Fresno peppers, seeded and finely diced

3 jalapeño peppers, seeded and finely diced

2 oz. cilantro leaves, finely chopped

1 lime

1 ½ cups rice wine vinegar

1 ½ cups granulated sugar

¼ cup sour cream

Wooden skewers, about 4-inches (soaked in water for 20 minutes)

SERVES 4

Peel and devein shrimp, discarding shells or reserving for another use. With a sharp knife, mince the shrimp, or alternatively pulse with food processer. Do not puree. In a mixing bowl, stir salt, paprika, minced shallots and half cilantro into shrimp mixture until well incorporated. With wetted hands, form shrimp mixture into 1 ½-inch round balls. To make gastrique, in heavy bottom saucepan, stir together sugar and vinegar and bring to a simmer. Reduce by ¼ on low heat. Add peppers to simmering vinegar and sugar reduction; steep off the heat for 10 - 15 minutes. Cool and set aside. Mix lime juice and sour cream together; add salt and pepper to taste.

Assemble by skewering 2 - 3 shrimp balls on wooden skewers and grill for 2 minutes on all sides or until done. Then, pour gastrique into a small bowl or shot glass. Place shrimp skewer atop gastrique dish. Add a small dollop of lime cream and garnish with paprika and a cilantro leaf.

SERVING SUGGESTION:
Enjoy with a unique variation on a margarita: The Bandalero, HANDCRAFTED COCKTAIL section.

KETCHUM GRILL ROCK SHRIMP CAKES

KETCHUM GRILL • CHEF SCOTT MASON • KETCHUM, IDAHO

The rock shrimp cakes are a standard at the Ketchum Grill in Ketchum, Idaho, adjacent to Sun Valley Resort. This popular menu selection has been featured on the menu since opening, under the inspiration of serving an alternative to the ubiquitous crab cake.

3 lbs. cream cheese, room temperature

2 lbs. rock shrimp, rinsed and drained

6 egg yolks

Butter

3 stalks celery, minced

2 medium onions, minced

¼ cup fresh dill, chopped

2 Tbsp. Tabasco sauce

1 tsp. white pepper, ground

4 - 5 cups Japanese bread crumbs

SERVES 6 - 8

EASIEST

In a sauté pan, melt butter and sauté onion and celery until translucent. Add Tabasco, white pepper and fresh dill. Mix together and set aside.

In a mixer equipped with a paddle, cream together cream cheese and egg yolks. Stir in celery and onion mixture. Coarsely chop rock shrimp and add to cream cheese mixture. Stir again until shrimp are incorporated with cheese. Reserve ½ cup of bread crumbs and mix in remaining crumbs to bind the cheese mixture. Chill mixture in refrigerator for at least 30 minutes.

Shape ½-inch thick silver dollar-sized cakes. Add remaining bread crumbs on outside to help cakes from sticking. Heat a sauté pan and add olive oil followed by shrimp cakes. Do not crowd the cakes in the pan or they will be hard to flip. Finished cakes can be held in a preheated oven while the others are cooking. Brown on one side, flip, reduce heat and cook until heated through (about 5 minutes). Shrimp cake batter can be prepared ahead of time and kept 2 - 3 days in the refrigerator.

SERVING SUGGESTION:

Serve shrimp cakes with a remoulade, tartar or aioli sauce beside a sparkling St. Germain Spritz cocktail, HANDCRAFTED COCKTAIL section.

THAI CHILI MUSSELS

NEW SHERIDAN CHOP HOUSE RESTAURANT • CHEF ERICH OWEN • TELLURIDE, COLORADO

At New Sheridan Chop House, you will feast on creations from classically trained chef Erich Owen in a cozy mountain setting. With Chef Erich's lofty resume, a skier can be guaranteed a one-of-a-kind culinary experience.

½ cup butter

2 Tbsp. fresh ginger, grated

4 shallots, minced

1 Tbsp. Mae Ploy Thai Red Curry Paste

2 stalks lemongrass, minced

1 bunch cilantro, chopped

4 whole Thai chilies

2 cups chicken stock

1 cup sake

1 can coconut milk

Serves 6 - 8

In a large pot, add ginger, shallots, lemongrass and Thai chilies along with butter. Sweat out and add sake. Reduce by half. Add mussels, chicken stock, coconut milk and red curry. Cover pot with lid. Steam for 5 minutes or until mussels fully open. Garnish with cilantro.

SERVING SUGGESTION:
While relishing the protein-rich mussels, sip a Pura Vida, HANDCRAFTED COCKTAIL section, for absolute gratification.

MODIS MUSSELS

MODIS • BRECKENRIDGE, COLORADO

In a vibrant, eclectic, happening atmosphere, Modis serves Colorado contemporary cuisine with an urban feel and a focus on the art of food and drink, like the pre-prohibition style cocktails.

2 strips bacon, diced

¼ cup fennel, julienned

2 large garlic cloves, thinly sliced

½ small jalapeño, thinly sliced

½ lb. PEI mussels, cleaned

¼ cup dry white wine

½ cup clam juice

¼ cup crushed tomatoes

1 Tbsp. mixed fresh herbs - parsley, oregano and basil

2 Tbsp. unsalted butter

S ERVES **2**

In a sauté pan, cook bacon until almost crispy, then remove from pan. Sauté fennel in remaining bacon fat until it begins to caramelize. Add garlic, jalapeños and reserved bacon and cook until garlic starts to brown on edges. Add mussels and immediately deglaze with wine. Add clam juice and tomatoes. Cover until mussels are cooked (about 3 minutes). Add herb mix and stir in butter until melted, then season with salt and pepper.

SERVING SUGGESTION:
Spoon mussels and glorious broth into a wide bowl. Garnish with chopped parsley and serve with baguette slices to savor the broth.

SWEET HOT MUSTARD

1 cup Dijon mustard

1 cup yellow mustard

1 cup whole grain mustard

½ cup brown sugar

¼ cup honey

¼ cup champagne vinegar

¼ cup Sriracha

Combine and blend all ingredients.

LOBSTER CORNDOGS
with Beet Aioli & Sweet Hot Mustard

BRANDING IRON GRILL • ALTA, WYOMING

While quite a bit of assembly, the homemade and elevated aspect of Lobster Corndogs with Beet Aioli and Sweet Hot Mustard, compared to a regular beef corndog with ketchup and mustard, is tremendously appetizing. Relish in the effort!

2 lbs. lobster meat, chopped

1 lb. raw scallops

1 lb. raw shrimp, peeled and tail removed

2 Tbsp. green onion, chopped

2 Tbsp. fennel, minced

2 Tbsp. shallots, minced

1 Tbsp. garlic, minced

½ cup heavy cream

1 Tbsp. salt

2 tsp. pepper

Sweet Hot Mustard

Beet Aioli

SERVES 6 - 8

MOST DIFFICULT

To create the lobster sausage, sweat fennel, shallots and garlic in a little oil on the stovetop. Cool. Puree seafood, cream, salt and pepper. Fold puree and sweated vegetables together. Using a pastry bag, pipe 1-inch diameter log into film wrap, making sure to force-out air. Then, twist ends to make sausage tight, and tie off ends. Continue making logs until mixture is depleted.

Place logs into boiling water and simmer 10 minutes. Take out of water and immediately place in ice water.

To assemble lobster corndogs, cut lobster sausages into ¾-inch segments. Stick with 6-inch wooden skewer. Fry in oil at 350 degrees until golden brown, turning once. Drizzle Sweet Hot Mustard and Beet Aioli on opposite sides of plate; arrange corndogs on mustard and aioli.

BEET AIOLI

1 quart mayonnaise

1 medium beet, peeled

1 tsp. garlic, minced

1 Tbsp. Dijon mustard

½ cup beet roasting liquid

½ tsp. salt

Roast beets in small pan with 1-inch of water and salt until tender. Puree beets with liquid while still hot, then cool. Combine all ingredients to create aioli.

SERVING SUGGESTION:
Garnish with arugula leaves tossed with salt and olive oil. For a final taste of the Northwest, sip a Huckltini cocktail, HANDCRAFTED COCKTAIL section.

CLANS
with Peppers, Saffron, & Tomato Confit

BROKEN TOP CLUB • CHEF PAUL ELLIS • BEND, OREGON

Once reserved only for club members, the Broken Top Club restaurant is now open to the public, offering the ultimate place to dine, drink and soak in the extraordinary Central Oregon scenery and sunshine. Chef Paul Ellis procures foods from Central Oregon and the Pacific Northwest that are of the highest quality: artisanal cheeses from Tumalo Farms, organic herbs and heirloom tomatoes from Klamath Falls, natural beef from Madras, natural poultry from Central Oregon and fresh fish from the coast are just some of the stellar ingredients.

2 Tbsp. oil

1 Tbsp. garlic, minced

1 lb. clams

¼ cup white wine

1 Tbsp. butter

Pinch crushed red peppers

Pinch saffron

Parsley, roughly chopped

2 Tbsp. Tomato Confit

SERVES 2 - 4

MORE DIFFICULT

In a saucepan, heat oil, garlic, clams and white wine. Cover and cook until clams are open. Add butter, crushed red peppers, saffron and parsley. Pour into bowl and top with Tomato Confit.

TOMATO CONFIT

4 cups tomatoes, diced

1 cup olive oil

½ cup basil, chopped

4 garlic cloves, crushed

Salt to taste

In a saucepan, combine all ingredients and cook over low heat until tomatoes are softened, about 20 minutes.

SERVING SUGGESTION:
This simply divine recipe pairs well with the Cinnamon Toast Crunch cocktail, HANDCRAFTED COCKTAIL section.

SMOKED TROUT BRUSCHETTA
with Braised Fennel, Capers & Meyer Lemon-Horseradish Crème Fraiche

SHORE LODGE • MCCALL, IDAHO

Dining is one of the main attractions at Shore Lodge for local guests, as well as visitors. A highlight of the dining experience is dinner at The Narrows, Shore Lodge's award-winning restaurant, which features a frequently changing menu. The Lake Grill serves a wide selection of favorite breakfast and lunch dishes. And, perhaps best known for its delicious range of gourmet burgers, The Narrows Grill and Game Room is the perfect place to unwind while enjoying a cocktail, light meal or snack and live entertainment after a day on the slopes.

2 Tbsp. extra virgin olive oil

1 head fennel, greens and root removed, thinly sliced

1 pint chicken stock or low sodium chicken broth

1 bay leaf

1 tsp. Meyer lemon zest

1 Tbsp. horseradish, ground

4 oz. crème fraiche or sour cream

Dash Worcestershire sauce

16 slices French baguette, ½-inch thick slices

Kosher salt

Pinch ground black pepper

6 oz. Idaho smoked trout, flaked

1 oz. capers

SERVES 6 - 8

MORE DIFFICULT

Heat 1 Tbsp. oil in medium sized sauté pan. Add fennel and cook, stirring occasionally, until lightly browned. Add chicken stock, bay leaf and a pinch of salt. Simmer over low heat until liquid has evaporated. Remove from heat and cool to room temperature.

In a mixing bowl, combine the zest, horseradish, crème fraiche and Worcestershire sauce. Refrigerate.

Preheat grill. Drizzle the baguette slices with remaining oil, and season with salt and pepper. Rest at room temperature for 10 minutes to allow oil to soak into bread. Char the bread and reserve.

To prepare Smoked Trout Bruschetta, arrange the charred baguette slices on a serving platter. Spoon a small amount of the crème fraiche mixture onto the bread, and top with 3 - 4 slices of the fennel. Finally, add a nice helping of the flaked trout and sprinkle with capers.

SERVING SUGGESTION:
The delicate bruschetta slices pair extraordinarily well with a Night Sky Over Payette Lake cocktail, HANDCRAFTED COCKTAIL section.

J & G GRILL'S TUNA TARTAR
with Spicy Avocado and Ginger Marinade

J & G GRILL AT THE ST. REGIS DEER VALLEY • PARK CITY, UTAH

A comfortable yet elegant hideaway, J & G Grill combines a curated selection of Jean-Georges' greatest appetizers, side dishes and accompaniments from his portfolio of domestic and international restaurants with the highest quality meats and freshest local fish. Simply grilled preparations accompanied by bold condiments anchor the J & G Grill dining experience at The St. Regis Deer Valley in a signature Jean-Georges' sophistication.

1 ¼ cups Ahi tuna, diced

1 Tbsp. olive oil

1 tsp. salt

½ tsp. Thai chili, minced

1 tsp. shallot, minced

¾ cup ripe avocado, mashed with salt to taste

4 radishes, thinly sliced

4 tsp. Chili Oil

½ cup Ginger Marinade

S E R V E S 4

MORE DIFFICULT

Toss tuna with olive oil then gently season with salt, shallots and Thai chilies; keep in a bowl over ice.

Place a 3-inch ring mold into the center of a cold appetizer bowl and spoon the mashed avocado into the bottom of the mold. Top with tuna. Arrange the sliced radishes on top, then drizzle each serving with 1 tsp. Chili Oil. Unmold the tartar and spoon the Ginger Marinade into the bowl.

CHILI OIL

1 Tbsp. Ancho chilies, seeded and toasted

1 tsp. dried chipotle chilies, seeded and toasted

½ tsp. allspice berries, toasted

½ tsp. cloves, toasted

1 ½ tsp. fennel seeds, toasted

1 tsp. mace, toasted

1 tsp. star anise, toasted

2 ½ tsp. cinnamon sticks, toasted

5 tsp. salt

1 cup grape seed oil

In a blender, puree all ingredients except oil until medium-fine. Add oil. Heat in a saucepan, stirring until 160 degrees. Let cool and strain, pushing for total extraction.

SERVING SUGGESTION:
Enjoy the tartar alongside the famous
7452 Mary, HANDCRAFTED COCKTAIL section.

GINGER MARINADE

¼ lb. ginger, peeled and roughly chopped

⅜ cup olive oil

1 ¼ cups champagne vinegar

1 ¼ cups soy sauce

¼ cup Kaffir Syrup

Puree ginger in a blender with olive oil, until totally smooth. Mix with remaining marinade ingredients.

KAFFIR SYRUP

½ cup lime juice

½ cup sugar

½ cup Kaffir lime leaves, washed and chopped

In a pot, combine all and heat to 190 degrees. Steep, covered, until cool.

LOBSTER CLAW PHYLLO BEGGARS PURSE

THE TOWER AT TALISKER CLUB • CHEF ROGER LAWS • PARK CITY, UTAH

Talisker Club's sous chef Roger Laws' style is described as an international and eclectic blend of traditional farm-to-table scratch cooking and premium Rocky Mountain fine dining. Members and guests at The Tower will notice hints of the Southwest, as well as influences from the Far East along with real attention to texture, big flavor and original presentation in his creations. His aesthetic might be a mouthful, but can be summarized in one word: balance. "To me," he says, "understanding the components of flavor is every chef's responsibility, but understanding balance and the techniques to achieve balance is what a chef really needs to do to put an amazing dish on the table."

1 pint lobster claw and knuckle meat, cooked

1 cup pine nuts, toasted

1 pint Gold Creek Farms feta cheese

1 cup blood orange, sectioned

1 quart wilted heirloom spinach

1 pint fresh heirloom spinach

1 Tbsp. Meyer lemon juice, freshly squeezed

16 #4 phyllo sheets (12 x 17-inches)

1 lb. unsalted butter

Many 12-inch chives, picked

Salt and pepper to taste

SERVES 8

MOST DIFFICULT

Before preparation, set aside a small amount of feta, pine nuts, blood orange sections and spinach for garnish.

In a mixing bowl, add pine nuts, feta, blood orange, spinach and lemon juice. Season with pepper and a very light dash of salt. Mix well and set aside.

Melt butter in a pan. Lay out two phyllo sheets, cut in half width-wise. Brush bottom layer with melted butter, lay the next layer on top and repeat until there are four layers saturated with butter. Divide the lobster meat into 8 equal portions. Mix one portion of lobster with about 1 cup of spinach mixture and create a tangerine-sized ball of filling.

Set the filling in the center of the phyllo and carefully pull up each corner to wrap the filling and create the purse. Pinch dough together with extra from the corners creating a rustic, flower shape of dough. Tie with chives at the neck. Repeat with remaining phyllo sheets, lobster and spinach mixture. This will create 8 phyllo purses.

Preheat oven to 300 degrees for convection oven and 325 degrees for non-convection oven. Place purses on non-stick sheet tray and bake for 10 - 12 minutes. Check progress and turn at 6 minutes. Remove when golden and crispy.

SERVING SUGGESTION:
Serve hot with a garnish of one shelled lobster claw, fresh heirloom spinach, crumbled feta, toasted pine nuts and blood orange sections. Enjoy the culinary greatness with an Aranciata Rossa Lemon Fizz cocktail, HANDCRAFTED COCKTAIL section.

EAST COAST MUSSELS
with Blood Orange Curry Butter, Marinated Tomatoes & Spicy Sausage

CROP BISTRO AND BREWERY • CHEF STEVE SICINSKI • STOWE, VERMONT

With his vast experience and versatile skills, Chef Sicinski (a Le Cordon Bleu graduate) is able to innovate well beyond cultivated and refined French cuisine. His innate understanding of the different industry facets prove why Crop Bistro and Brewery is where friends and family gather for sensational libations and delectable dining in a warm, inviting atmosphere.

3 lbs. East Coast blue mussels, rinsed and de-bearded

1 lb. spicy Italian sausage links, cooked and sliced

1 cup white wine

2 Tbsp. garlic, minced

1 Tbsp. olive oil

Blood Orange Curry Butter

Marinated Tomatoes

SERVES 6

 MORE DIFFICULT

Heat large sauté pan with oil. Add garlic and sausage before it gets hot; sweat slightly. Add mussels and wine, cover and steam over high heat. Mussels are ready when all are opened widely. Spoon into a large serving bowl and ladle plenty of Blood Orange Curry Butter over the top. Garnish with plenty of Marinated Tomatoes on top.

MARINATED TOMATOES

3 large tomatoes, neatly diced

1 bunch cilantro, finely minced

12 basil leaves, minced

20 chive sprigs, finely minced

2 Tbsp. rice wine vinegar

2 Tbsp. canola oil

Salt and pepper to taste

Combine tomatoes, herbs, oil and vinegar in large bowl. Season with salt and pepper; mix well. Reserve under refrigeration.

SERVING SUGGESTION:
Toasted baguettes are always recommended for soaking up the delectable liquid. Also, try pairing the mussels with a Mr. Figgy cocktail, HANDCRAFTED COCKTAIL section.

BLOOD ORANGE CURRY BUTTER

1 yellow onion, roughly chopped

3 garlic cloves, smashed

1 ¼ cups fresh ginger, peeled and chopped

1 cup blood orange puree or juice

2 Tbsp. turmeric

⅓ cup sweet chili sauce

1 quart heavy cream

½ lb. butter

2 Tbsp. yellow curry paste

¾ cup white wine

2 Tbsp. oil

Salt and pepper to taste

In a medium saucepan, heat oil over medium-low heat. Add onion, garlic and ginger; sweat over low heat until soft. Add white wine and orange puree; reduce by ¾. Add curry, turmeric and chili sauce; cook 3 minutes. Add cream and bring to a simmer, stirring frequently. Reduce by half. Blend ingredients in blender, small batches at a time. Add butter pat to each blended batch. Keep warm.

LOBSTER CRUDO
with Yuzo, Basil & Lime

LEONORA AT THE SEBASTIAN HOTEL • VAIL, COLORADO

Vail Mountain is the largest single resort in the United States with over 5,200 acres of the most diverse and expansive skiing in the world. Vail Mountain is accessed by three base areas: Lionshead, Vail Village and Golden Peak. Lionshead is home to the Eagle Bahn Gondola and Born Free Express. Mountain access out of Vail Village is via Vail's state of the art gondola, "One." Golden Peak is home to the Riva Bahn Express. Vail, Colorado is blessed with over 300 days of sunshine a year.

Maine lobster chunks

Yuzu Leche de Tigre

Serrano chili, thinly sliced

Avocado Purée

Micro basil

Extra virgin olive oil

Maldon sea salt

SERVES DESIRED PARTY SIZE

 MOST DIFFICULT Layer all ingredients in a glass serving dish, as this is a beautiful, fresh presentation.

AVOCADO PURÉE

2 avocados

1 lemon, juiced

2 Tbsp. extra virgin olive oil

Sea salt to taste

Place avocados in a blender and purée until a smooth paste. Season, then add extra virgin olive oil at the end while the blender is still running to emulsify. Taste; adjust seasoning and reserve.

SERVING SUGGESTION:
Serve with your choice of bread, vegetables or unaccompanied.

YUZU LECHE DE TIGRE

1 liter Basic Leche de Tigre

2 Tbsp. yuzu kosho or yuzu chili paste

Salt and pepper to taste

Combine both ingredients, season and blend well.

FISH FUMÉT

White fish bones, rinsed

1 tsp. white peppercorns

1 tsp. mustard seeds

1 sprig fresh thyme

1 bay leaf

Fish Fumét, also known as white fish broth, is prepared by placing fish bones in a pot with peppercorns, thyme, bay leaf and mustard seeds. Cover with ice and cold water and boil. Simmer for one hour and strain through fine mesh. Cool and reserve.

BASIC LECHE DE TIGRE

½ quart Fish Fumét (white, lean fish only)

¼ white onion

2 garlic cloves, peeled

½ ginger knob, peeled

½ stalk celery, peeled

4 oz. white fish, cured in lime juice for at least 4 hours

3 cilantro leaves

1 lemon, juiced

Salt and pepper to taste

Place all ingredients in a 2-inch pan. Pour the lime and lemon juice on top and let the whole thing macerate for at least 4 hours. Once the fish is cured, remove. Mix all the ingredients in a blender and purée until a nice creamy milk consistency. Strain through fine mesh and use to marinate ceviche.

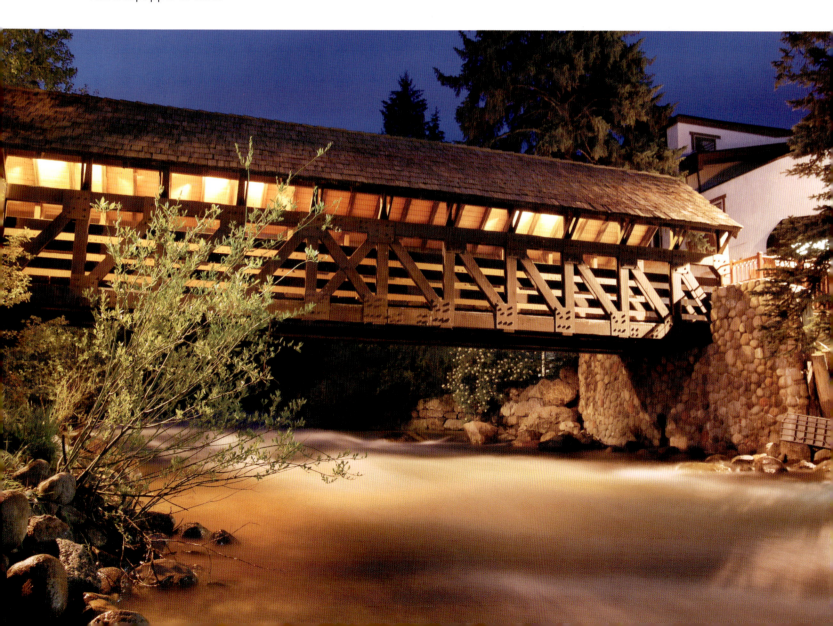

FRIED AVOCADO
with Old Bay Crab Salad & Green Goddess Dressing

TWIST • CHEF MATTHEW FACKLER • BRECKENRIDGE, COLORADO

Chef Matthew Fackler puts his own spin – an exciting, fresh take - on classic comfort food at Twist, examples being the Rueben Spiced Beef Meatloaf, the Braised Duck Ramen Noodle Bowl or the Juicy Lucy Elk Burger.

4 avocados, peeled, seeded and halved

1 cup flour

2 eggs

¼ cup milk

1 cup Panko breadcrumbs seasoned with 1 Tbsp. Herbs de Provence

3 cups canola oil

Old Bay Crab Salad

Green Goddess Dressing

SERVES 4

Heat canola oil in a steep-sided pot to 325 degrees. Mix eggs and milk together. Dredge avocados in flour, egg mixture and finally the breadcrumbs. Fry avocados in the oil until golden brown, approximately 3 - 4 minutes. Remove from oil and season with salt and pepper. Drain on paper towels and reserve. Dress a plate with a bed of greens and top with a couple fried avocadoes and a side of Old Bay Crab Salad. Then, drizzle with Green Goddess Dressing.

OLD BAY CRAB SALAD

1 lb. crab meat, cooked

½ yellow bell pepper, finely diced

½ red bell pepper, finely diced

½ red onion, finely diced

1 stalk celery, finely diced

1 Tbsp. olive oil

2 Tbsp. mayonnaise

2 Tbsp. crème fraiche

¼ cup chives, chopped

½ lemon, zested and juiced

1 tsp. Old Bay Seasoning

Sauté peppers, onions and celery in olive oil for 2 minutes, then cool. Combine with remaining ingredients.

GREEN GODDESS DRESSING

1 cup mayonnaise

1 cup crème fraiche

2 Tbsp. lemon juice

1 tsp. sherry wine vinegar

1 tsp. roasted garlic

5 - 6 anchovies

2 green onions, chopped

½ cup parsley leaves

¼ cup chives, chopped

¼ cup tarragon leaves

Salt and pepper to taste

Puree all ingredients together in a food processor until smooth.

SALMON TIRADITO
with Green Apple, Thai Curry & Jalapeño

LEONORA AT THE SEBASTIAN HOTEL • VAIL, COLORADO

A tiradito is a typical Peruvian dish, similar to a ceviche. Raw fish is cut into thin slices and flavored with a citrus sauce, in which the acidity cures the fish. A tiradito is simple yet elegant and delicious.

Salmon, thickly sliced

Red onion, thinly julienned

Jalapeño, thinly julienned

Green apple, thinly julienned

Green Curry Leche de Tigre

Micro cilantro

Extra virgin olive oil

Maldon sea salt

SERVES DESIRED PARTY SIZE

In a small dip dish, place some drops of extra virgin olive oil, then the Green Curry Leche de Tigre. Next, place the salmon slices on top of the sauce and garnish with apples, chilies, onions and fresh cilantro. Sprinkle with sea salt.

GREEN CURRY LECHE DE TIGRE

¼ cup wasabi paste

¼ bunch parsley

¼ bunch cilantro

¼ bunch spinach

1 Tbsp. Thai curry

1 jalapeño, seeded

1 cup green apple purée

¼ liter lemon juice

½ liter Basic Leche de Tigre (see Lobster Crudo, with Yuzo, Basil & Lime recipe in this section)

1 cup coconut milk

Kosher salt to taste

Combine all the ingredients in a blender and purée. Taste; season and strain through fine mesh.

SERVING SUGGESTION:
Serve with your choice of bread or crackers, or simply enjoy naturally.

TUNA WONTON TACOS

39 DEGREES LOUNGE AT THE SKY HOTEL • CHEF SHAWN LAWRENCE • ASPEN, COLORADO

At 39 Degrees Lounge, foodies enjoy social cuisine and notorious cocktails, not unlike the Tuna Wonton Tacos and Alpine Gem cocktail featured in this cookbook. Hailed as the hippest lounge in town and Aspen's most happening après-ski party, Sky Hotel's 39 Degrees defines modern swank with its seductive atmosphere, enticing locals and visitors alike.

1 package wonton skins, cut into large round shapes

1 tomato, diced

Sushi rice, cooked and cooled

Rice wine vinegar

Sugar

2 oz. Ahi (yellow tail) tuna, diced

Sesame seeds, toasted

Scallions, sliced

½ cup yuzu

¼ cup water

¼ cup soy sauce

1 tsp. sesame oil

Napa cabbage slaw, thinly sliced

Carrots, shredded

1 bunch cilantro, chopped

Tobiko, flying fish roe

Mayonnaise

Sriracha

Sweet soy sauce

3 avocados, peeled and seeded

2 limes, juiced

2 jalapenos, seeded

Pinch salt

Water

Mixed greens

Serves 2-4

MOST DIFFICULT

Prepare medium-grained sushi rice and season with rice wine vinegar and sugar to taste. Toss together cabbage, carrots and a bit of the cilantro. Set aside. Create marinade by mixing yuzu, water, soy sauce and sesame oil. Create avocado puree by blending together avocados, lime juice, jalapenos, cilantro, salt and a bit of water. In a small bowl, add a small amount of tomatoes, the diced tuna, sliced scallions, toasted sesame seeds and enough yuzu-soy marinade to coat.

To shape the wontons, use a small square mold and fold-up wontons to taco-shape. Heat oil to 375 degrees; fry shells until crispy. Drain on paper towels. Fill cooled shells with prepared rice, then some cabbage mix and finally the marinated tuna.

On a plate for serving, dollop some avocado puree and place the filled tacos on top of puree. Top each taco with Tobiko mayo. Add mixed greens in between each taco on the plate, then drizzle the plate and the tacos with the sweet soy and sprinkle with toasted sesame seeds. Top each taco with a fresh, small sprig of cilantro.

SERVING SUGGESTION:
Serve tacos with the Alpine Gem cocktail, HANDCRAFTED COCKTAIL section.

SHRIMP AL AJILLO
with Roasted Garlic, Salsa Verde & Red Chilies

LEONORA AT THE SEBASTIAN HOTEL • VAIL, COLORADO

Celebrated as one of the best tapas locations in Vail, Colorado, Leonora showcases a tapas platter unlike any other restaurant. The Shrimp al Ajillo is one of the tapas offerings at Leonora; they are delicately flavored with roasted garlic, red chilies and a bright, fresh salsa verde.

3 Tbsp. extra virgin olive oil

2 garlic cloves, thinly sliced

½ red chili (either guindilla or guajillo), chiffonade

2 cups ruby red shrimp

1 lemon, juiced

½ cup Italian flat-leaf parsley, finely chopped

Kosher salt to taste

Salsa Verde

Micro cilantro

SERVES **6**

Preheat sauté pan and add olive oil. Add sliced garlic and shrimp. Add the sliced red chilies and sweat for one minute. Remove from heat; add lemon juice and a small bunch of parsley. Taste and adjust seasoning.

SALSA VERDE

2 garlic cloves, blanched twice

1 cup Italian flat-leaf parsley

½ cup basil leaves

½ cup cilantro leaves

1 tsp. coriander seeds, toasted and ground in coffee grinder

1 tsp. cumin seeds, toasted and ground in coffee grinder

1 tsp. mustard seeds, toasted and ground in coffee grinder

1 Tbsp. capers

1 Tbsp. almond powder or toasted almonds, cooled down and ground

1 lemon, zested and juiced

¼ cup extra virgin olive oil, preferably Arbequina

Sel Gris de Guérande (gray salt) to taste

Place herbs in a blender, then add extra virgin olive oil, capers, lemon and spices. Blend until a smooth purée. Taste and adjust seasonings, if necessary. Reserve in a small squeeze bottle or container.

SERVING SUGGESTION:
On 6 small tapas plates, divide shrimp evenly and top with Salsa Verde and cilantro.

CHOPHOUSE OYSTERS ROCK

BEAVER CREEK AND VAIL CHOPHOUSE • CORPORATE CHEF JAY McCARTHY • AVON, COLORADO

Oyster Rockefeller is a classic oyster dish developed in New Orleans. Loving fresh oysters both summer and winter season at the Chophouse, a weekly oyster night was started - grilling oysters outside on the patio for a little summer version of après. Perfectly complimenting the freshly shucked oysters, the Rockefeller Mix is robust, dense and holds together nicely, especially paired with a flute of champagne. Throughout the winter season both the Vail and Beaver Creek Chophouse partake in a complimentary champagne toast at 3:30 pm daily. The tradition started as a celebration of 20 years of business in the Vail Valley and, more as a thank you to those who have supported The Chophouse along the way. Embarking on the 25th anniversary, the tradition continues.

6 raw oysters, shucked

¾ cup Chophouse Oysters Rock Spinach Artichoke Mix

2 Tbsp. Parmesan cheese, freshly and finely shredded

Chophouse Panko Crumb Topping

Rock salt, field greens and fresh lemon wedges (optional for presentation)

Serves 1 - 2

Arrange 6 oysters on a baking sheet. Top each with a spoonful of the Spinach Artichoke Mix. Sprinkle with Parmesan cheese. Place under a broiler, on high, until mix is heated through and cheese melts on top (approximately 6 minutes). While under the broiler, add a sprinkle of the Chophouse Panko Crumb Topping with 1 – 2 minutes remaining. Serve on a plate covered with rock salt to hold the hot oysters in place; garnish with mixed greens and lemon wedges on the side.

SERVING SUGGESTION:
Champagne makes a perfect pairing with either fresh or broiled Chophouse oysters, especially since the flute of champagne is "on the house" at The Chophouse.

CHOPHOUSE OYSTERS ROCK SPINACH ARTICHOKE MIX

2 Tbsp. garlic, peeled and minced (about 4 cloves)

2 Tbsp. shallots, peeled and minced (about 2 shallots)

1 Tbsp. white cooking wine

½ cup heavy cream

2 Tbsp. cream cheese

1 Tbsp. Parmesan cheese, grated

½ Tbsp. feta, crumbled

¾ cup artichoke hearts, drained, rinsed and coarsely cut

⅜ cup frozen spinach, drained, squeezed and chopped

In a dry pan, sweat garlic and shallots until shallots are clear (do not brown), about 3 minutes. Add white wine, heavy cream and cream cheese. Warm until cream cheese is smooth, about 3 minutes. Stir in remaining ingredients: Parmesan, feta cheese, artichoke hearts and frozen spinach. Stir until combined. This will make twice the amount of topping needed for 6 oysters and can be made ahead and reserved cold. The dip can be jazzed-up by adding jalapenos or roasted red peppers and can also be baked and served as a stand-alone dip.

CHOPHOUSE PANKO CRUMB TOPPING

1/4 cup Panko bread crumbs

1/4 cup Parmesan cheese, finely grated

1 Tbsp. parsley, finely minced

Mix together all ingredients.

NEW ORLEANS-STYLE ROASTED NOANK, CONNECTICUT OYSTERS

THE DOWNTOWN GROCERY • CHEF ROGAN LECHTHALER • LUDLOW, VERMONT

At The Downtown Grocery, Chef Rogan makes his own pastas, sources fresh, sustainable seafood and cures his own meats in the cellar beneath his casual, fine-dining eatery. His seasonal, regional cooking has been featured in The Wall Street Journal, GQ, Yankee Magazine *and* Outside Magazine. *He's also cooked at a private dinner party with Ashley Judd and Morgan Freeman, at an Ambassador's Dinner in Washington D.C. and at The James Beard House.*

12 oysters in the shell

½ cup pancetta or bacon, diced

1 cup Parmesan cheese, finely grated

1 Tbsp. pumpkin seeds, chopped and toasted

1 lemon, sliced

1 Tbsp. celery greens or chives, chopped

SERVES 3 - 4

 Set oven to broil. Clean oysters under cold water. Shuck oysters, taking care to keep as much of the flavorful liquid as possible inside each shell. Place oysters on a sheet pan with rock salt or a wet towel underneath to steady.

In a small pan, cook pancetta slowly on low heat until slightly crispy. Remove and drain on paper towels. Top oysters evenly with diced pancetta. Add grated Parmesan to each oyster. Roughly chop pumpkin seeds and toast in a separate pan, until beginning to brown.

Place sheet pan of oysters in oven for 4 - 6 minutes, or until golden brown. Remove oysters and top with chopped, toasted pumpkin seeds and chopped chives or celery greens.

SERVING SUGGESTION:
Garnish with sliced lemons and enjoy warm alongside a freshly shaken Vermont Vesper cocktail, HANDCRAFTED COCKTAIL section.

FRESH TUNA POKE

The Blacksmith Restaurant serves distinctively bold cuisine in a newly renovated, relaxed, yet ultimately elegant atmosphere. Along with the Tuna Poke on the extensive menu, a diner can enjoy the Roasted Mushroom Tart and Dungeness Crab Corndogs. Not to be overlooked, the cocktail list has been completely revamped to include unique libations, such as the Spicy Peach Lemon Drop.

1 cup Ahi tuna, diced

1 tsp. ginger, freshly grated

1 Tbsp. cilantro, chopped

1 Tbsp. shallots, diced

Pinch lime zest

1 tsp. salt

1 Tbsp. chili oil

1 Tbsp. fresh lime juice

½ tsp. soy sauce

Avocados, diced

SERVES 2

Assemble tuna, ginger, cilantro, shallots, lime zest and salt. On a plate drizzled with lime juice, chili oil and soy sauce, use a ring mold to shape tuna layer, then top with avocados.

SERVING SUGGESTION:
Serve with your choice of chips and a delicious Spicy Peach Lemon Drop cocktail, HANDCRAFTED COCKTAIL section.

LAND & TURF

SERVING SUGGESTION:
Drizzle meatballs with Mustard Dressing and serve alongside the Juniper Pickled Red Cabbage while sipping a
Huckleberry Bramble cocktail, HANDCRAFTED COCKTAIL section.

VENISON MEATBALLS

RUPERT'S AT HOTEL MCCALL • CHEF GARY KUCY • MCCALL, IDAHO

Owned and operated as an independent family hotel, the historic charm of Hotel McCall is the focal point of downtown McCall, Idaho. Locals and travelers will enjoy a spectacular meal at Rupert's within Hotel McCall, ranging from themes of Thai Night, Sunday Night Supper and Chef's Tasting Menu. Chef Gary Kucy is fast establishing himself as a notable and rising star in the culinary world as evidenced by his recent nomination for a James Beard Award for "Best Chef Northwest".

1 lb. ground venison

¼ lb. ground beef - 70/30

1 cup white onion, minced

1 Tbsp. garlic, minced

1 tsp. juniper berries, toasted and ground

2 tsp. fresh rosemary, chopped

2 eggs

⅓ cup bread crumbs

3 tsp. kosher salt

2 tsp. fresh ground black pepper

SERVES 4 - 6

EASIEST

In a large sauté pan, sweat onions and garlic until beginning to brown. Add juniper and rosemary; continue to cook for 1 – 2 minutes until fragrant. Remove from heat and cool.

In a large mixing bowl, mix together bread crumbs, eggs and cooled onion mixture. By hand, mix in meats, salt and pepper. Mix until well combined. Cook a small piece to check for seasoning and adjust, if necessary. Roll mixture into ½-ounce balls and place on cookie sheet. Slightly bake in oven for 5 minutes at 375 degrees to set meat. Skewer par-cooked meatballs on bamboo skewers (5 per 6-inch skewer). Cook over preheated grill until hot throughout, or meat thermometer reads an internal temperature of 155 degrees.

JUNIPER PICKLED RED CABBAGE

3 cups red cabbage, finely shredded

¾ cup apple cider vinegar

¼ cup sugar

¼ cup water

2 tsp. juniper berries, toasted and ground

1 tsp. rubbed sage

1 Tbsp. kosher salt

In a small bowl, season cabbage with salt and mix thoroughly. Set aside for 10 - 15 minutes until cabbage is softened. In a small saucepot, boil vinegar, water, sugar, juniper and sage. Once at a rolling boil, pour over salted cabbage and cool. Let mixture sit for 30 minutes or overnight. The cabbage will hold and improve with age for up to 7 days.

MUSTARD DRESSING

1 Tbsp. whole grain mustard

2 Tbsp. Dijon mustard

3 Tbsp. sherry vinegar

2 Tbsp. honey

4 Tbsp. olive oil

Whisk together all ingredients until well combined.

BONE-IN PORK CHOP
with Caramelized Onion & Apple Chutney

FOUNDRY AT SUMMIT POND • CHEF SEAN MILLER • KILLINGTON, VERMONT

In the heart of Killington, Vermont, on the banks of the Summit Pond, lies The Foundry, with its take on the traditional American Supper Club. The Foundry offers an American Bistro-Style menu in the formal dining room, as well as a casual Tavern menu in the bar. In addition to the impeccable, chef-driven cuisine and focus on hospitality in a warm and relaxing setting, The Foundry offers and hosts live entertainment and many of the area's events and activities on the pond – from ice-skating to the Killington Classic Motorcycle Rally.

2 bone-in pork chops, frenched

1 sweet onion, julienned

1 Tbsp. ginger root, minced

2 oz. Captain Morgan rum

2 Tbsp. whole grain mustard

1 cinnamon stick

2 cups apple juice

¼ cup brown sugar

¼ cup Vermont maple syrup – grade B

½ cup beef stock

2 Granny Smith apples, peeled and diced

2 Tbsp. sage, minced

Salt and pepper to taste

SERVES 2

 MORE DIFFICULT

Caramelize onions in a small amount of butter, then add ginger root and sauté for 1 minute. Deglaze pan with rum; add apple juice, cinnamon stick, whole grain mustard, brown sugar, maple syrup and beef stock. Bring to a boil, then lower heat to simmer and reduce by half. Add apples and sage and cook until chutney thickens.

Grill pork chops to 125 degrees, then let rest for 5 minutes.

SERVING SUGGESTION:
Serve the grilled pork chops with a good helping of chutney and a special Bulleit Proof cocktail, HANDCRAFTED COCKTAIL section.

ELK MEATBALL SLIDERS
with Mushroom Sauce & Arugula

THE AERIE RESTAURANT • SNOWBIRD, UTAH

After skiing the fresh powder at Snowbird Ski Resort or enjoying the "Greatest Snow on Earth" on a bluebird day, nothing satisfies like an open-face Elk Meatball Slider at The Aerie Lounge. Skiers can relax and watch the alpenglow on Mount Baldy, as evening shadows slip over Peruvian Gulch.

1 shallot, minced

2 garlic cloves, minced

½ lb. ground beef

2 lbs. ground elk

½ - ¾ cup panko bread crumbs

2 eggs

¼ cup cream

2 Tbsp. fresh parsley, chopped

1 Tbsp. fresh thyme, chopped

1 Tbsp. fresh rosemary, chopped

3 tsp. salt

1 ½ tsp. black pepper

Mushroom Sauce

Baguette, sliced and toasted

Dried shallots

SERVES 4 - 6

Preheat oven to 350 degrees. Mix all ingredients (except Mushroom Sauce, baguette slices and dried shallots) together and season. Make a tester meatball to make sure the seasoning is correct. Form mixture into 2 oz. balls. Cook on a sheet pan with a little bit of water on the bottom of the pan in a 350-degree convection oven, about 12 - 15 minutes. Serve Mushroom Sauce over the top of the meatballs on toasted baguette slices with arugula on top. Garnish with dried shallots.

MUSHROOM SAUCE

3 Tbsp. olive oil

1 shallot, minced

½ cup sherry wine

2 cups mixed mushrooms (button, shiitake and crimini), sliced

3 cups vegetable stock

2 cups cream

1 Tbsp. fresh parsley, chopped

1 Tbsp. fresh thyme, chopped

1 Tbsp. fresh rosemary, chopped

Salt and pepper to taste

In a medium saucepan, heat oil over medium heat and sweat shallots until translucent. Add mushrooms and cook until caramelized. Deglaze with sherry. Add vegetable stock and cook until reduced by half. Add cream, and cook until reduced by half. Season with herbs, and salt and pepper to taste.

SERVING SUGGESTION:
Pair with a cold Snowbird Dunkelweizen, which highlights flavors of banana, clove and toasty malt merged with sweet caramel and a hint of cocoa.

GRILLED QUAIL
with Potato Cakes, Chutney & Apple Gastrique

JACK CREEK BAR AND GRILLE • BIG SKY, MONTANA

No matter what time of year a visit to Big Sky is planned, Moonlight Basin will entertain all in your party. The Moonlight Basin snow sports are a point of pride, while wine tastings and culinary exhibits are not uncommon either. In the summer, peace and tranquility of yoga can be found on an outside deck, or horseback riding in the Gallatin National Forest.

4 quails

3 Yukon Gold potatoes, grated

1 medium shallot, minced

3 garlic cloves, minced

2 apples, peeled and diced into ¼-inch cubes

½ lb. pancetta, ¼-inch cubes

¾ cup walnuts, lightly toasted

1 quart apple cider

1 cup apple cider vinegar

Salt and pepper to taste

Canola oil

SERVES 4

MORE DIFFICULT

In a medium-size pot, add apple cider and vinegar and bring to a simmer. Slowly reduce the liquid to ½ cup; it will have a syrup-like consistency. Heat medium-size frying pan, cook pancetta until crispy. Remove pancetta and set aside in a bowl. Sauté shallots and garlic until tender. Add apples and cook until just done. Put aside and keep warm.

For potato cake, season potatoes with salt and pepper. Heat a large frying pan and add enough canola oil to coat the pan well. Form cakes into four 3-inch disks and crisp potatoes in pan until golden brown on both sides.

Oil and season quail with salt and pepper. Grill quail until medium (slightly pink on the inside). Place potato cake on a plate; top with quail. Spoon chutney on top of quail and drizzle the apple gastrique over quail.

SERVING SUGGESTION:
Beside the fire, enjoy this fall/winter-inspired dish with a glass of Cristom's 2011 Mt. Jefferson Pinot Noir.

VENISON BRUSCHETTA
with Morel Confit & Stuffed Morel Tempura

MORELS AT TAMARACK AND DELISH CATERING • CHEF SHANNON BERRY • TAMARACK, IDAHO

Aiming to bring the Idaho experience to clients, Delish Catering continues to research local resources and bring wonderfully fresh items from Idaho and the northwest region to showcase a culinary tour of Idaho. This reputation led to Delish Catering becoming the operators for the fine dining aspect of Tamarack Resort's restaurant, Morels at the Lodge at Osprey Meadows.

Crusty baguette

Herbed soft cheese

Venison tenderloin - Black Pine Deer Farm sourced

Roasted red peppers

Morel mushrooms, fresh or dried

Gorgonzola cheese - Idaho Litehouse

Tempura batter

Milk

1 shot brandy

Shallots

Butter

Olive oil

SERVES 4

Soak mushrooms in milk and brandy, then cut mushrooms into rounds and sauté with shallots and butter. Season venison tenderloin and grill to rare, then slice on the bias. Cut baguette into 8 - 10 thin crostini, spread with olive oil and lightly toast. Spread a thin coat of herb cheese on one side of crostini. Place one tenderloin slice atop each crostini; crisscross 2 strips roasted red pepper atop venison. Finally, top with crumbled Gorgonzola and sautéed morels. Caramelize under broiler for a minute until cheese bubbles slightly and mushrooms are crisp.

To create Morel Tempura, stuff remaining morels with herb cheese, coat in tempura batter and deep fry until golden brown. Place on a bed of greens in middle of bruschetta serving platter.

SERVING SUGGESTION:
Enjoy the food of Idaho with a drink of Idaho: I'm Your Huckleberry Martini, HANDCRAFTED COCKTAIL section.

VERMONT CAVENDISH FARMS QUAIL KABOB
with Romesco Sauce & Watercress Salad

EPIC RESTAURANT • CHEF JASON TOSTRUP • LUDLOW, VERMONT

After tutelage of some of the best chefs in New York, Chef Jason Tostrup constructed a simple culinary philosophy: "do what's right for the land, the animals and the food that's produced from it." Chef Jason is known as a leader in New England's farm-to-table movement and has developed strong alliances with area growers and producers. His culinary expertise has wide-range, and is showcased in this Spanish-style "Tapas" appetizer featuring locally sourced quail from Cavendish Game Birds of Vermont. This zippy, tasty finger food is a great way to nourish yourself and share moments with your skiing companions after an epic day.

16 Vermont quail legs

4 quail eggs

1 bunch watercress

4 radishes, sliced

4 bamboo skewers

¼ cup chives, chopped

Romesco Sauce

SERVES 4

 MORE DIFFICULT

Season quail legs with salt and pepper. Place four legs per skewer. Bake in oven for 12 minutes at 425 degrees. Remove from oven and toss with Romesco Sauce and chives. Using a non-stick pan, fry quail eggs sunny-side up. Place watercress and radishes on base of a plate, then top with quail kabobs and cooked eggs. Drizzle with more Romesco Sauce and chopped chives.

ROMESCO SAUCE

¼ cup olive oil

1 cup garlic, chopped

Piquillo peppers

¼ cup Marcona almonds

¼ cup sourdough bread

1 garlic clove, chopped

1 tsp. coriander seed

1 Tbsp. sweet smoked paprika

1 Tbsp. sherry vinegar

3 Tbsp. extra virgin olive oil

1 Serrano pepper, chopped

Salt and pepper to taste

Heat small saucepot over medium and add olive oil. Add garlic and sauté for 1 - 2 minutes. Add remaining ingredients; simmer for 10 - 15 minutes. Place sauce in a blender and puree until smooth. Season with salt to taste.

SERVING SUGGESTION:
A Grey Goose Lemon Citron Bloody Mary with Vegetables, HANDCRAFTED COCKTAIL section, pairs well with these kabobs.

CARAMELIZED ONION AND JALAPEÑO MIX

3 Tbsp. olive oil

2 medium yellow onions, sliced into thin rings

2 fresh jalapeños, seeded and sliced into thin rings

Salt and pepper to taste

1 – 2 pinches sugar

Splash white wine

Heat oil in a heavy pan. Add onions, jalapeños, sugar, salt and pepper. Cook over medium heat until onions are caramelized. Deglaze with a splash of white wine.

ELK MEATLOAF SLIDERS
with Caramelized Onions and Jalapeños

THE BACK BOWL SOUP COMPANY • WINTER PARK, COLORADO

Owners Jodi and Steve "Woody" Johnson state that the onion mixture is key to these sliders. When these sliders or full sandwiches are offered as an unadvertised weekly special at The Back Bowl Soup Company, they are sold out within an hour once word spreads. These are also perfect for a Broncos game day snack.

Meatloaf, ½-inch slices

Ciabatta rolls

Butter

Caramelized Onion and Jalapeño Mix

Smoked provolone

Horsey Mayo or prepared horseradish mayo

SERVES 6 - 8

Slice meatloaf into ½-inch pieces and brown on a cast iron skillet on one side. Slice ciabatta rolls, butter and toast on a cast iron skillet until brown and crispy. Spoon a large portion of Caramelized Onion and Jalapeño Mix on meatloaf and cover with a slice of local smoked provolone. Cover the pan until cheese melts. Spread Horsey Mayo (or prepared horseradish mayo) on rolls and add meatloaf slices, slightly overlapping.

MEATLOAF

2 lbs. ground elk meat

2 links Italian pork sausage, casings removed

1 medium onion, finely diced

1 large green bell pepper, finely diced

2 medium eggs

2 cups dried bread crumbs (add dried oregano and basil, if preferred)

1 ½ cups milk

½ cup ketchup, reserve ¼ cup for top

2 Tbsp. prepared mustard

Salt and pepper to taste

Crumble elk and sausage, add all other ingredients (save ¼ cup ketchup) and gently knead until mixed. Form into a loaf in a bread pan, then top with additional ketchup. Bake at 350 degrees until internal temperature reaches 165. Place in refrigerator to chill.

HORSEY MAYO

¼ cup hot horseradish

¾ cup mayo

Mix ingredients. Reserve in refrigerator.

SERVING SUGGESTION:
Enjoy warm on a cold day.

AJAX DOUBLE CHEESEBURGER

AJAX TAVERN AT THE LITTLE NELL • ASPEN, COLORADO

The Ajax Double Cheeseburger is a celebrated and beloved dish that is served with truffle fries at Ajax Tavern. The tavern is conveniently located at the base of Aspen Mountain, so the sundrenched mountainside patio is an idyllic hotspot for casual fine-dining in an unbeatable atmosphere.

1 burger bun – from Louis Swiss Pastry

6 oz. Milagro Ranch grass fed beef, formed into 2 thin patties

⅛ head romaine lettuce, shredded

2 slices vine-ripened tomato

1 oz. Double Double Sauce

2 slices Kraft American cheese

Salt and pepper to taste

SERVES 1

Toast bun in whole butter to golden brown. Season both sides of patties with salt and pepper. Grill 3 minutes on a side, then flip and add cheese to melt. Remove bun from pan; place on cutting board. Spread Double Double Sauce on top side, and add lettuce and tomato. Assemble by placing patties on bottom side and closing. Wrap in paper and secure with a toothpick.

DOUBLE DOUBLE SAUCE

2 cups 1000 island dressing

1 large yellow onion, julienned

1 oz. Tabasco sauce

1 tsp. butter

Caramelize onions in butter. Blend and mix with 1000 island dressing and Tabasco.

SERVING SUGGESTION:
Serve with French fries or another favorite side, as Ajax Tavern serves with truffle fries and enjoy a
Drop the Beet cocktail, HANDCRAFTED COCKTAIL section.

ELK CROSTINI
with Huckleberry Goat Cheese

FORMERLY OF JOHN'S ANGELS CATERING • LAKESIDE, MONTANA

Elk Crostini looks elegant and tastes delicious, especially combined with the additions of tart huckleberry preserves and tangy goat cheese. Make the elk roast a day or two beforehand, then use the leftovers for this easy-to-assemble appetizer.

Crusty bread, 2-inch slices

Braised elk, leftovers

Huckleberry preserves or jam

Goat cheese or cream cheese

Fresh parsley

Salt and pepper to taste

SERVES DESIRED PARTY SIZE

EASIEST

Lightly toast rustic bread slices. Spread huckleberry preserves or jam and goat cheese on crostini. Thinly slice elk roast to fit crostini. Season with salt and pepper, and top with fresh parsley.

ELK ROAST WITH VEGETABLES IN A RED WINE BRAISE

Extra virgin olive oil

2 cups shallot or sweet onion, chopped

2 cups carrots, chopped

1 cup celery, chopped

1 cup fennel, chopped

½ cup leeks (white parts only), chopped

Whole baby potatoes

2 bottles red wine (preferably not Cabernet)

8 cups beef stock (preferably homemade)

Fresh herbs (your choice: thyme, rosemary, sage and/or oregano)

5 - 8 lbs. elk roast

4 pats butter

Preheat oven to 425 degrees and season elk with salt and pepper on all sides. Put a little olive oil in a pan and sear elk on all sides until browned. Transfer to a lidded-roasting pot or Dutch oven large enough for all ingredients. You can even use a crockpot, adding baby potatoes the last 45 minutes of cooking. In sauté pan, add all vegetables and sauté until slightly tender, about 8 minutes. Add 1 bottle wine, fresh herbs, and boil until liquid reduces by half. Add 4 cups stock and reduce again. Pour remaining mixture over elk. Add remaining stock and wine until the elk is ¾ covered. Reserve unused liquid, for use in pot if liquid reduces too much. Cover and put in oven for 3 ½ - 4 hours. Add potatoes with 45 minutes of cooking left. If using a crockpot, watch liquid reduction. When elk is done, remove and rest while making sauce. Set whole potatoes aside for a side dish; strain liquid by pushing juices out of vegetables. Use salt and pepper, if necessary. Add more wine to liquid, if you don't have enough liquid and reduce on stovetop to approximately 3 cups. Remove from heat; add butter to finish your sauce. Slice roast against the grain and serve with red wine sauce and potatoes. Reserve elk roast for Elk Crostini with Huckleberry Goat Cheese.

SERVING SUGGESTION:
Enjoy the simple assembly.

BUFFALO CHEESESTEAK SPRING ROLLS

ASCENT LOUNGE AT FOUR SEASONS RESORT • TETON VILLAGE, WYOMING

Reflecting the historic Western heritage of Jackson Hole, the Four Seasons Resort dining establishments pair distinctive flavors with casual elegance, creating an inviting atmosphere. A large stone fireplace, dynamic open kitchen and stunning views of Teton Village and Rendezvous Peak provide a cozy, dining setting.

1 lb. buffalo flank steak

1 cup caramelized onions

1 cup Poblano peppers, roasted and julienned

½ cup cilantro, chopped

1 cup mozzarella cheese, shredded

1 cup pepper jack cheese, shredded

1 package spring roll wraps

½ cup egg wash

Salt and pepper

SERVES 4

MORE DIFFICULT

Thinly slice uncooked buffalo flank steak against the grain (easiest by freezing for a little while). In roasting pan over medium heat, add caramelized onions, Poblano peppers and buffalo flank steak; cook through. Remove from heat and add cilantro and both cheeses; stir and season to taste. Place mixture on sheet pan and let cool for 1 hour in refrigerator.

Remove wrappers from package and place one sheet down on a clean cutting board, then spread egg wash on corners with pastry brush. Place one more wrapper atop and add 2 ounces buffalo cheesesteak mixture. Roll into a spring roll, and continue process with the rest of the mixture. Cover spring rolls with plastic wrap and place in refrigerator or freeze. To cook, heat fryer oil up to 350 degrees and fry until golden brown.

SERVING SUGGESTION:
The perfect Buffalo Cheesesteak Spring Rolls pair well with The Perfect Gentleman,
HANDCRAFTED COCKTAIL section.

ELK CARPACCIO
with Bulgur Tabbouleh Salad and Mustard Aioli

CHEF KELLY LIKEN • VAIL, COLORADO

Kelly Liken, one of Colorado's most promising and influential young chefs, recalls, "From the moment I stepped foot into a professional kitchen, I knew it was where I wanted to be…it was like an epiphany." Chef Kelly has been recognized with three James Beard Award nominations for "Best Chef Southwest" and with features in Food & Wine *Magazine,* Bon Appétit *and* 2008 Women Chefs: The Next Generation. *She has also appeared on the* Food Network's Iron Chef America, NBC's TODAY Show *and has been a contestant on* Bravo's Top Chef D.C.

½ Tbsp. coriander, toasted and ground

½ Tbsp. fennel seed, toasted and ground

½ Tbsp. mustard seed, toasted and ground

Salt and pepper to taste

2 lbs. elk loin, cut in half lengthwise

Tabbouleh Salad

Mustard Aioli

S ERVES **8**

Mix coriander, fennel seed and mustard seed with salt and pepper for spice rub. Rub loins with spice mix. Sear loins in a very hot pan, so loins stay rare. Wrap loins in plastic (in cylindrical shapes) and freeze. Once frozen, slice loins very thin and arrange on baking paper in a flower pattern.

To serve, flip a parchment arrangement onto a plate. Top with a scoop of Tabbouleh Salad and finish with a drizzle of Mustard Aioli, salt and pepper.

SERVING SUGGESTION:
Enjoy this dish with a refreshing cocktail from Kelly Liken.

TABBOULEH SALAD

½ cup bulgur

1 ¼ cups water

½ cup parsley, finely chopped

2 Tbsp. mint, finely chopped

1 ½ cups tomato, peeled, seeded and brunoised

¾ cup cucumber, brunoised

2 Tbsp. lemon juice

1 garlic clove, minced

¼ cup extra virgin olive oil

Salt and pepper to taste

Boil water and stir in bulgur; cover and turn off heat. Let stand 25 minutes until most of the liquid is absorbed and bulgur is fluffy and tender. Drain and rinse bulgur under cold water. Whisk lemon juice, garlic, olive oil, salt and pepper together. In a bowl, combine bulgur, herbs, vegetables and dressing and mix until just combined. Cover and store in the cooler.

MUSTARD AIOLI

1 egg yolk

1 cup blended oil

½ lemon, juiced

3 Tbsp. whole grain mustard

Salt and black pepper to taste

Water, to thin if needed

Whisk egg yolk, lemon juice and mustard. Slowly incorporate oil in a thin stream while whisking constantly. Season to taste and thin with water, if necessary, for proper consistency.

ROASTED RADISHES

2 Tbsp. butter

4 radishes

Salt and pepper

In sauté pan, add butter and sliced or quartered radishes. Brown over high heat until radishes are golden. Season with salt and pepper.

SMOKED GRASS-FED LAMB RIBS

THE SUNFLOWER • CHEF KALON WALL • CRESTED BUTTE, COLORADO

The Sunflower is a communal kitchen – a progressive concept where a group of food and coffee-loving, long-time locals teamed up to share a restaurant space and resources. Chef Kalon Wall, along with a couple other chefs, delivers scrumptious farm-to-table suppers.

1 lamb rib

1 shallot

2 Tbsp. olive oil

1 bay leaf

3 juniper berries

10 whole white peppercorns

4 whole black peppercorns

1 quart lamb stock

1 cup alder wood chips

Salt and pepper to taste

Spring Onion Soubise

Green Garlic Giardiniera

Roasted Radishes

SERVES 2 - 4

Season lamb rib with salt and pepper and olive oil. Marinate for 30 minutes. Smoke lamb with alder chips for 1 hour. Once meat is roasted golden, place in roasting pan with lamb stock, shallots, bay leaf, juniper berries and white and black peppercorns. Bring liquid to a boil and cover. Braise in oven 275 degrees for 3 hours or until meat is tender; let rest in liquid.

Once lamb has rested in pan, cover and return to heat until lamb and drippings sauce is warm. Place Spring Onion Soubise on bottom of plate, sprinkle with Roasted Radishes and rest lamb atop. Ladle lamb drippings over meat and top with Green Garlic Giardiniera.

SPRING ONION SOUBISE

½ cup butter

6 oz. spring onions

Salt to taste

Combine butter with spring onions in pot, bring to low simmer for 1 hour until onions are very soft. Put mixture in blender with salt to taste and blend until smooth. Keep warm.

GREEN GARLIC GIARDINIERA

½ cup green garlic

¼ cup salt

½ cup hot water

½ cup cold water

¼ cup Banyuls wine vinegar

2 sprigs marjoram

1 Tbsp. honey

Thinly slice garlic. Combine salt and hot water until salt is dissolved. Add cold water. Pour salt water over garlic and marinate for 1 hour. Rinse garlic with cold water. Combine wine vinegar, honey and chopped marjoram. Add to rinsed garlic. Set aside.

SERVING SUGGESTION:
Enjoy this very decadent, elegant dish with a glass of wine.

BISON TARTAR

YELLOWSTONE CLUB • CHEF ROB WALTZ • BIG SKY, MONTANA

Yellowstone Club is authentic Montana – a private, residential community brings to life all the treasures of a very special mountain resort. In the only private ski resort in the world, owners explore spectacular beauty and the benefits of membership in this exclusive one-of-a-kind club. Chefs at Yellowstone Club blend authentic Montana cuisine, including delectable wild game dishes, with menus that include comfort foods and classic club fare.

1 tsp. white anchovy, chopped

1 tsp. sweet onion, grilled

1 tsp. capers, chopped

½ tsp. strong Dijon mustard

¼ tsp. white truffle oil

2 Shisito peppers

1 bunch micro watercress

Lemon juice

1 quail egg

Crostini, toasted

6 oz. bison tenderloin, diced

Salt and pepper to taste

SERVES 2 - 4

In a mixing bowl, combine bison, mustard, truffle oil, capers, onions, anchovy and salt and pepper. Blend watercress with lemon juice and water to create a smooth emulsion. Press bison mixture in a steel ring mold, top with a quail egg and serve with crostini. Dress plate with watercress emulsion and drizzle with olive oil.

SERVING SUGGESTION:
Enjoy this ultimate example of Montana cuisine with another Montana treat: a Huckleberry Limeade cocktail, HANDCRAFTED COCKTAIL section.

ROCKY MOUNTAIN GAME PLATTER

WHITEHORN LODGE • LAKE LOUISE, ALBERTA

Located at 6700 feet above sea level, Whitehorn Lodge is the perfect spot for a variety of food items such as cheese fondue, signature seafood chowder, the Rocky Mountain game platter or a house-made bison burger. Newly renovated, Whitehorn Lodge is designed to be the showcase of full service dining at the ski area, where guests are invited to enjoy sweeping panoramic views and fantastic scenery while experiencing an upscale menu in a casual environment.

Cheeses of your choice

Smoked meat of your choice

Salami of your choice

Baguettes

Crackers

Fruit of your choice

Sweet, hot and/or stone ground mustard

SERVES DESIRED PARTY SIZE

EASIEST

Assemble a sampler platter containing ingredients of your choice.

SERVING SUGGESTION:
With meats and cheeses, a Bloody Mary cocktail of your choice is truly divine.

PARKER PASTURES BEEF TARTAR

THE SUNFLOWER • CHEF KALON WALL • CRESTED BUTTE, COLORADO

There are few places remaining that can be called true Colorado ski towns. Crested Butte is considered a holdout, retaining its small town charm and adventurous soul. People openly celebrate life every day; the genuine nature of the community and the pristine surroundings capture everyone.

4 oz. beef round, from Parker Pastures

4 radishes, shaved

Quail egg

3 Tbsp. olive oil

Salt and pepper

Spring Onion Soubise*

Green Garlic Giardiniera*

SERVES 1 - 2

Cut beef round into thin strips, then cross cut the strips. Continue chopping beef until the texture is that of ground beef. In mixing bowl, season beef with 1 Tbsp. olive oil, salt and pepper; mix well.

In a small sauté pan over low-medium heat, add 1 Tbsp. olive oil with one quail egg. Cook sunny side up for 1 minute - white should be cooked while leaving the yolk runny.

On a plate, place Spring Onion Soubise, and top with chopped and seasoned beef in appropriate ring mold. Add sunny side quail egg. Combine radishes with Green Garlic Giardiniera, olive oil, salt and pepper and add to plate.

* See Smoked Grass-Fed Lamb Ribs recipe in this section for additional recipes.

SERVING SUGGESTION:
Like Crested Butte, let this dish capture and entice you with a glass of your favorite wine.

UTAH LAMB MEATBALLS

STEIN ERIKSEN LODGE • CHEF ZANE HOLMQUIST • PARK CITY, UTAH

Lamb is a ubiquitous dish to the western states: Colorado and Utah, especially. Using tender, young lamb will keep away from the flavor that does not appeal to most. Traditionally, lamb was served with a mint jelly or sauce, but gourmets have branched out to serving lamb in a plethora of fashions.

2 lbs. ground lamb

2 garlic cloves, crushed and minced

1 shallot, finely chopped

½ cup Mizithra or Feta cheese, grated

4 Tbsp. extra virgin olive oil

½ cup pretzels, ground

1 tsp. cumin

1 Tbsp. fresh oregano, chopped

3 Tbsp. fresh parsley, chopped

½ lemon, zested

1 Tbsp. kosher salt

1 tsp. black pepper

SERVES 6

Combine meat, garlic, shallots, cheese, olive oil, pretzels and spices in a large bowl. Mix thoroughly by hand, being careful not to over-mix. Roll mixture into 1 ½-inch uniform meatballs. Evenly space meatballs on a non-stick sheet. Cook at 350 degrees for approximately 13 - 15 minutes, being carful not to overcook. Remove from oven.

SERVING SUGGESTION:
Serve Utah Lamb Meatballs with Swedish Mashers and top with warm World Famous Chow-Chow.

GRANDMA HOLMQUIST'S SWEDISH MEATBALLS & LINGONBERRY SAUCE

STEIN ERIKSEN LODGE • CHEF ZANE HOLMQUIST • PARK CITY, UTAH

Swedish meatballs and lingonberry sauce is a traditional dish in Scandinavian cuisine. Lingonberry jam, relish or sauce is used to adorn beef stew or liver dishes, but may also be sampled with fried herring. In North America, lingonberries are also known as mountain cranberries or partridge berries.

1 ½ lbs. ground pork

1 ½ lbs. veal

½ yellow onion, finely diced

3 Tbsp. fresh parsley, finely chopped

3 Tbsp. honey

2 eggs, beaten

¼ cup bread crumbs

1 tsp. black pepper

2 tsp. kosher salt

¼ tsp. nutmeg

¼ tsp. allspice

Lingonberry Sauce

SERVES 8

Combine all ingredients in a bowl; mix thoroughly by hand being careful not to over-mix. Roll into 1 ½-inch uniform balls. Evenly space meatballs on a non-stick sheet pan. Cook at 350 degrees for 18 - 20 minutes until meatballs are cooked through.

Remove meatballs from oven and place in Lingonberry Sauce to serve.

LINGONBERRY SAUCE

8 oz. lingonberry jam

3 cups veal demi-glaze (available in specialty food stores)

¾ cup heavy cream

2 Tbsp. arrowroot or cornstarch

4 Tbsp. cold water

Combine lingonberry jam, reduced demi-glaze and heavy cream in a saucepan; simmer. Combine cornstarch with cold water to make a slurry. Whisk slurry into the sauce mixture while it is simmering. It will begin to thicken after adding the slurry. Continue to simmer until sauce is a gravy-like consistency.

SERVING SUGGESTION:
Enjoy the European taste of these meatballs and sauce.

PARKER PASTURES BEEF ROULADE

THE SUNFLOWER • CHEF KALON WALL • CRESTED BUTTE, COLORADO

A perfectly fresh addition to a spring meat dish, Spring Onion Soubise, Green Garlic Giardiniera and Roasted Radishes are added to this beef roulade for a burst of flavor and aesthetic presentation.

4 oz. beef round, from Parker Pastures

1 cup butter

3 Tbsp. olive oil

4 oz. mustard greens, blanched

1 Tbsp. stone ground mustard

Butcher twine

Salt and pepper to taste

Spring Onion Soubise*

Green Garlic Giardiniera*

Roasted Radishes*

SERVES 4 - 6

 Thinly slice beef into 2 oz. pieces, pound if necessary. Lay flat on cutting board and season meat with salt and pepper. Spread thin layer of mustard atop, then top with blanched mustard greens, making a thin layer on top of meat. Take closest side of meat and roll away, curling meat on top of itself until a rolled log forms. Using butcher twine, tie 3 loops around roulade, securing meat into its form. Over high heat, smoke 1 Tbsp. olive oil in sauté pan and add roulade. Brown for 30 seconds on all sides; remove from heat and let rest on plate. Once meat has rested for 2 minutes, slice into 1-inch medallions.

To plate, put Spring Onion Soubise on plate first, then lay beef medallions on top. Place Roasted Radishes next to beef and top with Green Garlic Giardiniera. Finally, drizzle the dish with olive oil.

* See Smoked Grass-Fed Lamb Ribs recipe in this section for additional recipes.

SERVING SUGGESTION:
This dish is splendid with a favorite glass of wine.

ELK MEATBALLS & CHIPOTLE BBQ SAUCE

ASCENT LOUNGE AT FOUR SEASONS RESORT • TETON VILLAGE, WYOMING

Known as the living room at Four Seasons Resort Jackson Hole, Ascent Lounge is an intimate and comfortable bar and restaurant with a sleek, Western look. Guests enjoy expansive views of Rendezvous Mountain and the coziness of the lounge's wood-burning fireplace from comfortable couches and chairs or outside on the heated patio. One of the most popular and ideal bars and après-ski destinations in Jackson Hole, it boasts an east meets west inspired menu with selections from flat breads to udon noodles and a delicious list of specialty cocktails.

3 lbs. ground elk

1 cup white bread crumbs (soaked in milk)

1 cup garlic puree

1 cup rosemary and parsley, chopped

4 egg yolks

Salt and pepper

Chipotle BBQ Sauce

Serves 10 - 12

Mix all ingredients together. Cook a sample to taste for correct seasoning. Form mixture into 1 oz. meatballs. Oil sheet pan and roast at 350 degrees for 10 minutes. Macerate in Chipotle BBQ Sauce.

CHIPOTLE BBQ SAUCE

3 oz. chipotle peppers, pureed

1 cup shallots, caramelized

2 Tbsp. roasted garlic puree

½ cup red wine vinegar

1 cup roasted red bell pepper, pureed

½ cup ketchup

½ cup honey

½ cup Worcestershire sauce

Mix all ingredients and simmer for 20 minutes.

SERVING SUGGESTION:
Elk Meatballs are lovely served on a bed of sautéed kale with a Wyomatoe Bloody Mary cocktail, HANDCRAFTED COCKTAIL section.

ELK MEATBALLS

SNOWMASS KITCHEN AT THE WESTIN SNOWMASS RESORT • SNOWMASS, COLORADO

Snowmass Kitchen exceeds your expectations, from a packed breakfast buffet to the fast and fresh pizza/pasta lunch buffet, and then the Northern Italian themed menu for dinner.

32 oz. ground elk

3 Tbsp. garlic, minced

2 eggs

1 cup Parmesan cheese

2 Tbsp. parsley, chopped

1 cup Panko breadcrumbs

1 ½ cups half and half

½ cup yellow onions, finely chopped

1 Tbsp. paprika

1 Tbsp. oregano

2 tsp. onion powder

Arrabbiata Sauce

Serves 8 - 10

In a mixing bowl, place all ingredients. Mix on slow speed for 2 minutes, until incorporated. Refrigerate for 4 hours, then form meatballs into 1 oz. size. Roast in a 425-degree oven for 8 minutes. Fold into Arrabbiata Sauce.

ARRABBIATA SAUCE (SPICY MARINARA)

6 Tbsp. extra virgin olive oil

2 cups yellow onions, small diced

1 ¼ cups red bell peppers, small diced

1 ¼ cups yellow bell peppers, small diced

⅝ cup garlic, small diced

Burgundy wine

2 Tbsp. red chili flakes

Tomato paste

1 plum tomato

4 Tbsp. tarragon

In a sauté pan, add oil and sweat diced vegetables. Add rest of ingredients and simmer for 1 hour. Puree together and adjust seasoning with salt, if needed.

SERVING SUGGESTION:
Try devouring the meatballs with a Rx Renewal cocktail, HANDCRAFTED COCKTAIL section.

HOUSE CURED DUCK "CUBANO"

Traditionally, the Cubano sandwich is a variation on a "ham and cheese." However, former Flame chef Jason Harrison's miniature Cubano sandwiches are anything but traditional. These concoctions are elevated with the house-cured duck breast, decadent duck confit and the salty pretzel buns.

1 Duck Breast Ham, thinly sliced

Duck Confit

5 pretzel breadsticks, sliced in half lengthwise and cut to make 3 mini buns

30 slices baby cucumber, pickled

15 slices Gruyere cheese, sliced to match bun size

Violet mustard (available at specialty stores)

SERVES 6 - 8

Toast pretzel bread on both sides, cut side down, until golden brown. Spread a thin layer of violet mustard on the top buns and add sliced pickles. Place duck ham on bottom buns, then place confit on top and cover with a slice of Gruyere. Place bottoms of the sandwiches under a broiler until cheese is melted and meat is warmed through. Combine the two halves of the sandwich and serve immediately.

SERVING SUGGESTION:
This hearty sandwich is perfect unadorned.

DUCK BREAST HAM

1 duck breast

1 pint water

9 tsp. salt

2 ½ tsp. sugar

1 tsp. pink salt

3 Tbsp. maple syrup

3 Tbsp. Madeira

1 sprig thyme

2 bay leaves

1 Tbsp. juniper berries

Combine all ingredients, except duck, and bring to a boil, then cool down. Once cooled, add duck breasts. Cover and cure in solution for 12 - 16 hours. Remove duck from solution and rinse. Let dry uncovered in the refrigerator on a cooling rack for 8 hours. Smoke cured breast to an internal temperature of 160 degrees. Cool, remove skin and reserve.

DUCK CONFIT

¼ cup kosher salt

1 bay leaf, broken into pieces

1 Tbsp. fresh thyme, chopped

⅛ cup Italian parsley leaves

1 shallot

1 lemon, zested

2 cloves

2 allspice berries

½ tsp. black peppercorns

3 8-oz. whole duck legs

3 cups rendered duck fat, melted

In a spice grinder, blitz salt, bay leaf, thyme, parsley, peppercorns, cloves and allspice until well combined and a vivid green color. Place legs flesh side up on rack over a sheet tray. Cover legs completely in salt mixture. Cover legs with plastic wrap and refrigerate for 24 hours.

Melt down duck fat and completely submerge cured legs. Place a piece of parchment over the top and cover with plastic wrap and foil. Cook in a 210-degree oven for 10 - 12 hours, or until meat pulls away from the bone and is

very tender. Remove from oven and cool completely while still submerged in the fat. If possible, allow confit to sit for 1 - 2 days before using.

Slowly heat fat mixture up enough to remove the legs. Pull meat from bones, taking care to leave meat in nice chunks.

BACKSIDE STOUT SMOKED RIBS

STEAMWORKS BREWING • DURANGO, COLORADO

The name Purgatory, as Durango Mountain Resort was formerly known, comes from a witty farmer who lived in the area during the late 1800s. He adopted the moniker for a nearby creek, a tributary of the Rio de las Anima Perdidas (the River of Lost Souls), dubbed by Spanish explorers for a group who disappeared on the river during Durango's early history. Durango Mountain Resort is a destination where wildflowers grow thick as grass, trails lead off into the sunset and family members come to reunite.

3 racks St. Louis ribs

BBQ Sauce

Rib Rub

SERVES 6 – 8

MORE DIFFICULT

Rub meat with Rib Rub the night before smoking ribs. Prepare smoker by heating to 215 degrees. Smoke ribs for about 5 hours. While ribs are smoking, prepare BBQ Sauce. Baste ribs with BBQ Sauce 45 minutes before the ribs are done and then again when they are finished.

SERVING SUGGESTION:
Serve with extra BBQ Sauce. A cold Steamworks Brewery Backside Stout is a perfect combination with these smoked ribs.

BBQ SAUCE

1 Tbsp. olive oil

¼ cup yellow onion, diced

1 Tbsp. garlic, minced

2 cups ketchup

½ cup Steamworks Brewery Backside Stout

1 ¾ tsp. curry powder

2 tsp. coarsely ground pepper

2 ½ Tbsp. corn syrup

4 Tbsp. brown sugar

5 Tbsp. molasses

2 ½ tsp. liquid smoke

¾ cup water

¼ tsp. ground cinnamon

Sauté onions and garlic in olive oil until onions are translucent. Add remaining ingredients and simmer over low heat for 20 minutes. Makes 1 quart of BBQ Sauce.

RIB RUB

⅓ cup coarsely ground pepper

¼ cup paprika

2 Tbsp. sugar

1 Tbsp. kosher salt

1 Tbsp. chili powder

1 Tbsp. garlic powder

Combine rub ingredients and set aside.

SMOKED BBQ PULLED PORK SLIDERS

SUNSET GRILLE AND BAR • CHEF M. MATHISEN AND CHEF TIFFANY NASH • MESA, COLORADO

The Sunset Grille and Bar is a cafeteria-style restaurant featuring comfort food with a western flair. Like guests who proclaim Powderhorn as a "hidden gem," the Smoked BBQ Pulled Pork Sliders were inspired to highlight the great products from the Western Slope of Colorado and to continue that "Aha moment" for guests.

6 – 8 lbs. pork shoulder

¼ cup kosher salt

2 ½ cups Dr. Pepper

¼ cup brown sugar

12 slider buns, toasted

Cole Slaw

SERVES 6 - 8

MORE DIFFICULT

Rub pork shoulder with kosher salt and brown sugar. Place pork shoulder in baking pan and add Dr. Pepper. Cook for 15 hours at 225 degrees. Cover after 4 hours. Pork shoulder will be very tender and you will be able to pull it apart. On one slider bun, place 3 – 4 oz. pulled pork. Top with 1 – 2 oz. Cole Slaw.

COLE SLAW

1 head green cabbage, shredded

1 head purple cabbage, shredded

5 carrots, shredded

2 onions, diced

¼ cup apple cider vinegar

2 ½ cups mayonnaise

¼ cup prepared yellow mustard

⅛ cup canola oil

2 cups white sugar

1 tsp. salt

Mix all ingredients together in large mixing bowl. Chill for 2 hours.

SERVING SUGGESTION:

The Mad Mike Fizz cocktail, HANDCRAFTED COCKTAIL section, is refreshing and offers a good balance to the sweet pulled pork.

185

BUFFALO CHICKEN LEGS

FORMERLY OF SCANLON'S • BEND, OREGON

In 1928, winter sports in the Cascades began when Scandinavian lumber workers who came to central Oregon from the Great Lakes States and from Europe, formed the Bend Skyliners Mountaineering Club. Owned by Powdr Resorts, Mt. Bachelor recently opened an eighth high-speed detachable quad with 13 new runs and 630 acres of new intermediate and advanced terrain.

12 chicken legs

½ cup olive oil

½ cup onion, chopped

¼ cup celery, chopped

¼ cup carrots, chopped

1 Tbsp. garlic

2 bay leaves

1 tsp. crushed red pepper

1 Tbsp. thyme

1 cup red wine

1 quart chicken stock

Hot Wing Sauce

Blue Cheese Dressing

SERVES 4 - 6

MORE DIFFICULT

In a heavy saucepan, heat olive oil and add chicken legs seasoned with salt and pepper; sear brown on all sides. Remove chicken from pan and add onions, celery, carrots, garlic and cook until soft. Add bay leaves, red pepper flakes, and thyme; cook for 5 minutes. Add wine, chicken stock and browned chicken legs. Bring to a boil then reduce to a simmer. Cook until leg meat is starting to fall off the bone. Remove from heat and let chicken legs cool in liquid.

Heat oven to 350 degrees. Toss cooled chicken legs in Hot Wing Sauce and heat thoroughly.

HOT WING SAUCE

1 cup Cholula

1 Tbsp. butter

Heat until butter is melted.

BLUE CHEESE DRESSING

1 cup non-fat Greek yogurt

1 Tbsp. dry ranch seasoning

3 Tbsp. blue cheese crumbles

Incorporate all ingredients together.

SERVING SUGGESTION:
Serve legs with Blue Cheese Dressing, carrots, celery and a Ruby Dream cocktail, HANDCRAFTED COCKTAIL section.

BEEF YAKATORI

DOUBLE BLACK NOODLE BAR AT WILDWOOD SNOWMASS • SNOWMASS VILLAGE, COLORADO

Double Black Noodle Bar offers unique noodle bowls ready to tempt taste buds with a variety of fresh herbs and vegetables. Imaginative dishes include the Beef Yakatori, which is a commonly used term meaning a Japanese type of skewered beef.

Beef tenderloin scraps, large diced

Garlic, chopped

Onion, chopped

Soy sauce

Black pepper

Bamboo skewers

Spicy Cilantro Sauce

S ERVES DESIRED PARTY SIZE

EASIEST Marinate beef in garlic, onion, soy sauce and black pepper. After a few hours of marinating, skewer beef onto bamboo skewers that were previously soaked in water. (About 2 oz. per skewer.) Grill skewers, medium-rare to medium. Arrange on a plate with Spicy Cilantro Sauce on the side.

SPICY CILANTRO SAUCE

2 Tbsp. ginger, chopped

1 Tbsp. garlic, chopped

3 Kaffir lime leaves

5 jalapenos, chopped

3 cups salad oil

1 cup rice vinegar

½ lb. cilantro

2 Tbsp. Sambal

1 Tbsp. salt

Puree all ingredients in a blender for 2 minutes. Set aside.

SERVING SUGGESTION:
Try sampling the Beef Yakatori with a Wild and Spicy Margarita, HANDCRAFTED COCKTAIL section.

LOCAL RUSTIC CHICKEN
with Spring Garnish

JOHN HARVARD'S BREW HOUSE • CHEF BRIAN KIENDL • ELLICOTTVILLE, NEW YORK

John Harvard's Brew House is THE spot for great après ski in Ellicottville. Just steps from the slopes with tables facing a grand view of the mountain, the atmosphere is always lively and friendly. Classically trained Chef Brian Kiendl prepares comfort food with an eclectic twist and fresh, inspired, New American cuisine.

7 oz. chicken breast (skin on, wing attached)

Chicken drumstick (bone exposed)

Butter-poached Egg Yolk

Spring Garnish

SERVES 2

 In a pan, roast all chicken, so skins turns golden. In a 375-degree oven, finish cooking chicken. Arrange all chicken, Spring Garnish (cauliflower puree, english peas, greens and mini florets) and Butter-poached Egg Yolk in a serving plate, as shown.

SERVING SUGGESTION:
Enjoy this spring-tasting dish with a Hendricks McTwist, HANDCRAFTED COCKTAIL section.

BUTTER-POACHED EGG YOLK

3 large free range chicken eggs

2 lbs. clarified butter

Heat butter to 180 degrees. In mixing bowl crack all 3 eggs. Very gently, using slotted spoon, seperate yolk from white. Carefully place in butter. Repeat twice with other two eggs. Remove yolk from butter when it has developed a hard skin around the edge, but still has a running center.

SPRING GARNISH

1 head cauliflower

Salt

2 oz. whole milk

¼ lb. butter

Mini cauliflower florets

Spring onions, charred and slivered tops

Spring peas

Tendrils from the pea plant

Arugula

Micro spinach

Endive

Fresh basil

Wild spearmint

10 pods of english peas

Break down cauliflower head into quarter-size florets. In a pot, place in cold water to cover with a splash of milk and salt to season. Cook until completely fork tender; remove cauliflower and place into a blender. Add a pinch of salt and 2 ladles of cooking liquid. Puree and add half the butter.

Carefully pick all greens and herbs and place in a bowl of ice water to refresh. Reserve and drain before placing onto the plate.

Toss mini cauliflower florets with olive oil and salt.

Remove English peas from pod. Place in a pot of boiling, salted water until completely cooked and vibrant green. Remove from pot and immediately place in ice water to stop the cooking process.

HERITAGE BREED PORK BELLY STEAM BUNS
with Crispy Brussel Sprout Kimchi Slaw

FLAME RESTAURANT AT FOUR SEASONS RESORT VAIL • VAIL, COLORADO

Framed by dramatic vaulted, beamed ceilings inspired by Vail Mountain, Flame at Four Seasons Resort Vail celebrates the iconic American steakhouse with perfectly seared prime steaks and locally sourced, seasonal specialties. This recipe was created by the former chef of Flame Restaurant, Chef Jason Harrison.

½ lb. Sous Vide Pork Belly, cut into ¼-inch thick slices

1 pint Brussel Sprout Kimchi Slaw

12 steam buns

SERVES 6

Place buns into a steamer basket and steam for 3 minutes, or until warmed through, soft and pliable. Pan-sear sliced pork belly until crispy and warmed through. Deglaze with pork jelly that remains in the bag. Assemble pork buns by placing two slices of belly on the bottom and top with Brussel Sprout Kimchi Slaw.

SERVING SUGGESTION: These small sandwiches yield perfect bites.

PORK BELLY

¼ cup kosher salt

¼ cup sugar

2 cups water, divided

½ lb. skinless boneless pork belly, cut into quarters

Combine salt, sugar and water in a small pot over medium heat, stirring until sugar and salt have dissolved. Vacuum seal the pork belly in brine and marinate for 24 hours.

Remove pork from brine and pat dry with a hand towel. Vacuum seal the belly on 99% and cook sous vide at 170 degrees for 10 hours. If the home cook does not have sous vide equipment, using a pot fitted with a candy thermometer is a great way to try the sous vide technique without a big investment.

Remove and let chill in an ice bath; hold cold until ready for assembly.

BRUSSEL SPROUT KIMCHI SLAW

1 quart brussel sprouts, chiffonade

1 cup carrots, julienned

1 cup daikon radish, julienned

¼ cup Kimchi Dressing

Deep fry brussel sprouts until crispy and beginning to brown, about 30 seconds. Combine all ingredients in a mixing bowl and toss to coat evenly.

KIMCHI DRESSING

⅛ cup daikon radish, shredded

½ Tbsp. salt

⅛ cup sugar

⅛ cup ancho powder

5 slices ginger

5 garlic cloves

2 Tbsp. fish sauce

2 Tbsp. soy sauce

½ cup scallion, minced

1 lime, juiced

1 Tbsp. shallots, finely chopped

½ cup water

Combine daikon, sugar, chili powder, ginger, garlic, fish sauce, soy sauce and water; stir. Add scallions and allow flavors to combine for at least 24 hours. Puree in a blender, adding filtered water if necessary, until it forms a smooth sauce that coats the back of a spoon.

AVOCADO, FARM EGG & PORK BELLY

MOODY'S BISTRO, BAR & BEATS • TRUCKEE, CALIFORNIA

Boasting a Zagat-rated menu and wine list, a meticulously assembled live music lineup and a classic lounge-inspired setting, Moody's is simply a see-for-yourself dining staple with a menu crafted to please an afternoon snacker or a sit-down diner.

½ avocado, seeded

1 pork belly

2 cups salt

2 cups granulated sugar

Celery, chopped

Onions, chopped

Carrots, chopped

1 farm egg

2 cups beer and chicken stock

Crostini

Béarnaise Sauce

Salt and pepper to taste

S ERVES 1 - 2

Wrap pork belly, salt and sugar in plastic and cure for 3 days. Rinse. Roast pork belly at 450 degrees on bed of mirepoix (a mixture of celery, onions and carrots) until golden brown. Submerge pork belly in beer/chicken stock mixture. Braise at 300 degrees for 4 hours. Scoop out center of avocado, enough to crack egg into avocado half. Bake at 450 degrees until egg is cooked to preferred temperature. Remove avocado meat from skin after baking with egg. Portion pork belly and heat by roasting at 500 degrees until crispy.

Place avocado with egg on plate with pork belly and crostini. Drizzle Béarnaise Sauce over top and season with salt and pepper to taste.

BÉARNAISE SAUCE

1 lb. butter, melted and cooled

4 egg yolks

Shallot

Tarragon

Black pepper

White wine

White wine vinegar

Cook and reduce shallot, tarragon, pepper, wine and vinegar to opaque. Strain reduction and whisk-in egg until the mixture doubles in size. Add butter slowly while whisking. Add water, if needed, to thin sauce. Reserve sauce.

SERVING SUGGESTION:
Moody's Bloody Mary, HANDCRAFTED COCKTAIL section, is perfectly suited for this appetizer.

SERVING SUGGESTION:
Garnish with peanuts, Pickled Green Apple and Squash Slivers, scallions and fresh cilantro. Find Frost's
Steamed Buns recipe at: www.skitownlife.com

PORK BELLY BAO

FROST BAR AT THE SEBASTIAN HOTEL • VAIL, COLORADO

Pork Belly Bao is especially good because of the accompaniments: plum sauce, pickled green apple and squash slivers and homemade steamed buns. Feel free to simplify the recipe by purchasing buns.

Steamed buns

Plum Sauce

Pickled Green Apple and Squash Slivers

Bamboo leaves, optional

Micro cilantro

Scallions for garnish

Peanuts, toasted and roughly chopped

Pork belly (center cut)

Peanut oil

Dark soy sauce

SERVES 8

Bring a Dutch oven or heavy-bottomed pot of water to a boil. Add pork belly and simmer for 30 minutes. Remove from the pot, rinse under cold water and then dry with some paper towels. Slice pork into 3 even pieces and set aside.

Heat wok over high heat and add peanut oil. When oil begins to smoke, add pork pieces and stir-fry for 1 minute per side to brown. Add dark soy sauce and stir-fry for 2 minutes. Transfer pork to a plate that will fit inside a large steamer, then steam on plate over a wok or pot filled halfway with boiling water. Steam pork over medium heat until pork is tender, 1 – 1 ½ hours. Make sure water does not evaporate.

Remove pork from steamer and transfer all juices from pork into a small wok or pan. Slice pork belly. Brush each piece with the Plum Sauce and fill each steamed bun with a slice of pork and more Plum Sauce.

PLUM SAUCE

1 Tbsp. ginger, grated

1 Tbsp. oyster sauce

1 Tbsp. hoisin sauce

1 Tbsp. dark soy sauce

3 Tbsp. sugar

1 cup water

1 Tbsp. peanut oil

1 onion, chopped

1 Tbsp. cornstarch

2 Tbsp. sesame oil

Combine first six ingredients. Make a slurry with cornstarch and 1 Tbsp. cold water. Heat a wok over medium-high heat and add peanut oil. When hot, add onion; stir-fry until soft. Add sauce mixture and boil. Stir slurry into mixture, thickening for 30 seconds. Add sesame oil. Cool in refrigerator.

PICKLED GREEN APPLE AND SQUASH SLIVERS

Butternut squash, peeled and sliced in ribbons or julienned

Green apples, peeled and sliced in ribbons or julienned

1 cup water

½ cup chardonnay or white wine vinegar

½ cup sugar

1 Tbsp. salt

1 star anise

1 clove

4 black peppercorns

You can use a mandolin to slice squash and apples. Boil remaining ingredients and cool. Strain out aromatics. Immerse squash and apple in separate sealed bags or glass jars with enough pickling liquid. Pickle for 24 hours.

SERVING SUGGESTION:
Enjoy the tacos with a Legendary Caesar cocktail, HANDCRAFTED COCKTAIL section.

DUSTY'S KOREAN PULLED PORK TACOS

DUSTYS BAR & BBQ • WHISTLER, BRITISH COLUMBIA

The Korean Pulled Pork Tacos on Dusty's menu are representative of Fusion BBQ with a twist! The famous, fan-favorite pulled pork is served as "build your own taco" with traditional Korean BBQ sauce, Sambal mayo, coleslaw and fresh grilled corn tortilla.

16 – 18 lbs. boneless pork shoulder

2 cups Dusty's Butt Rub or another pork rub

2 cups Dusty's Korean BBQ Sauce or another BBQ sauce

1 cup apple juice

Corn tortillas

SERVES A LARGE PARTY

MORE DIFFICULT

Rub pork shoulder with 1 cup rub. Smoke with apple wood chips for 14 hours or until pork pulls apart easily. Shred shoulder into a large mixing bowl. Toss shredded meat in remaining rub, Korean BBQ Sauce and apple juice. Serve hot with Sambal Mayo, Korean Slaw and fresh, grilled corn tortillas.

KOREAN BBQ SAUCE

1 cup Gochujang (a Korean red pepper paste)

1 ½ cups white sugar

1 cup soy sauce

3 Tbsp. rice vinegar

6 Tbsp. sesame oil

Whisk all ingredients together until sugar dissolves. Keep refrigerated.

SAMBAL MAYO

2 cups mayo

3 Tbsp. sambal oelek (hot sauce)

1 smoked jalapeno, seeds, stem and pith removed

1 Tbsp. garlic puree

1 lemon, juiced

Salt and pepper to taste

Mix all ingredients together.

KOREAN SLAW

1 head green cabbage, thinly sliced

2 medium size carrots, peeled and shredded

1 long English cucumber, peeled, seeded and thinly sliced

2 cups green onion, chopped

1 cup cilantro, chopped

1 cup soy sauce

⅓ cup rice vinegar

8 tsp. garlic, minced

3 Tbsp. ginger powder

3 Tbsp. white sugar

Salt and pepper to taste

Whisk all dressing ingredients until sugar dissolves. Toss vegetables in an appropriate amount of dressing and refrigerate for 20 - 30 minutes. Toss again before serving.

WAGYU BEEF STREET-STYLE TACOS

FROST BAR AT THE SEBASTIAN HOTEL • VAIL, COLORADO

These street-style, casual tacos are misleading – there is nothing "casual" about the sophistication of Wagyu beef with Grilled Pasilla Chile Salsa, and cilantro and lime embellishments. You can also change-up the flavors using grilled fish, chopped lobster or other meat choice.

Wagyu beef, small cubes

Vegetable oil

Salt and pepper to taste

Grilled Pasilla Chile Salsa

Corn tortilla, warmed

Cilantro leaves

Lime wedge

SERVES DESIRED PARTY SIZE

SERVING SUGGESTION:
Serve with a side of the splendid salsa and corn chips, if desired.

 MOST DIFFICULT

Sauté beef in vegetable oil, season with salt and pepper and serve over warm corn tortillas. Top with Grilled Pasilla Chile Salsa, fresh cilantro and alongside a lime wedge.

GRILLED PASILLA CHILE SALSA

3 Tbsp. blended oil

1 white onion, peeled, quartered and grilled until charred

1 head garlic, halved and grilled until charred

10 hot-house tomatoes, peeled, washed and grilled until charred

2 red peppers, washed and grilled until charred

2 dried pasilla chilies, toasted on grill and rehydrated in warm water

1 dried morita chile, toasted on grill and rehydrated in warm water

1 dark beer (Negra Modelo, preferably)

½ cup cilantro, chiffonade

1 Tbsp. smoked chipotle, puréed

1 lemon, juiced

Kosher salt to taste

Extra virgin olive oil to taste

Yields 1 ½ quarts

Grill onions, garlic, red peppers and tomatoes. Grill all dried chilies then rehydrate them in warm water. Preheat a medium-size pot. When warm, add blended olive oil.

Add all the ingredients and sauté for a couple minutes. Pour in dark beer and simmer for 25 minutes, or until most liquid evaporates. Blend briefly to a rustic salsa consistency. Transfer to a bowl and finish with the chipotle puree, cilantro and lemon juice. Taste and season well; finally, drizzle extra virgin olive oil.

TAMARACK SLIDERS
with Bourbon Bacon Onion Relish

UNBUCKLE AT TAMARACK • CHEF BOB OFFERLE • SOUTH LAKE TAHOE, CALIFORNIA

Unbuckle at Tamarack, rated as the No. 1 après ski party in North America by Forbes *and confirmed by* CNN Travel *as Lake Tahoe's highest elevation après ski party featuring music, drinking, dancing and the lovely Heavenly Angels - ripping skiers by day and go-go dancers when the sun dips below the Sierras. Tamarack Lodge chefs have tailored food offerings for the après ski appetite, and bartenders at Bar 9150 mix up the ultimate cocktails to kick off the evening.*

1 lb. fresh ground beef - 85/15

1 Tbsp. steak seasoning

2 slices Ghost pepper jack cheese, quartered

½ cup Bourbon Bacon Onion Relish

8 slider buns, freshly baked

Lettuce

Tomato, sliced

Onion, sliced

SERVES 4

 MORE DIFFICULT

Mix steak seasoning in ground beef. Form 8 patties and place on hot grill, flipping after 4 minutes. After flipping once, top cooked side with 1 Tbsp. Bourbon Bacon Onion Relish then with pepper jack cheese. Toast buns on grill. When cheese is melted and bun is toasted, place slider on bun with lettuce, tomato and onion.

SERVING SUGGESTION:
Serve these mouth-watering sliders with a Mountain Mary cocktail, HANDCRAFTED COCKTAIL section, and garlic fries.

BOURBON BACON ONION RELISH

1 lb. gourmet bacon, cut into half lengthwise, then ½-inch pieces

2 large sweet onions, thinly sliced

½ cup packed light brown sugar

½ cup bourbon

¼ cup balsamic vinegar

1 Tbsp. kosher salt and black pepper

In a large pot over medium heat, cook bacon until crisp. Remove with a slotted spoon and reserve excess bacon grease. Place sliced onions in pot and cook 8 - 10 minutes, stirring until the onions start to soften and become translucent. Stir in brown sugar, salt and pepper. Cook for 10 - 15 minutes until onions start to caramelize. Stir in bourbon, balsamic vinegar and ¼ bacon. Cook for 10 minutes. Turn off heat and cool for 20 - 30 minutes. Strain and reserve all the liquid.

Place reserved liquid and about ¼ of the bacon-onion mixture into a blender. Pulse until pureed consistency, then pour over non-pureed bacon-onion mixture. Stir and refrigerate in an airtight container.

WOOD-GRILLED ORGANIC EGG
with Heirloom Hominy, Brown Butter, Pork Jowl Confit & Cacio Pecora

BEANO'S CABIN • CHEF BILL GREENWOOD • AVON, COLORADO

This simple "egg dish" is elevated by the creamy hominy and delicious pork jowl confit. It is very representative of the uniqueness and Rocky Mountain cooking style that Chef Bill and Beano's Cabin showcase. To simplify this grandiose recipe, you can use canned hominy. Chef Bill rates this recipe as "advanced," but suggests that it is simpler than one would imagine.

Fruition Farms Cacio Pecora or Reggiano cheese, thinly sliced

½ lemon

Hominy, cooked

Grilled Organic Egg

Pork Jowl Confit in brown butter

Kosher salt and cracked black pepper

SERVES 3

Spoon hominy on bottom of bowl, place a Grilled Organic Egg on top, place Pork Jowl Confit next to egg and spoon brown butter around dish. Lay cheese slice on top, squeeze lemon over dish and add a pinch of salt and pepper.

PORK JOWL CONFIT

1 lb. Tender Belly pork jowl

2 cups canola oil

2 tsp. kosher salt

1 Tbsp. whole black peppercorns

3 sprigs thyme

3 garlic cloves, crushed

¼ lb. butter, browned

Place all ingredients, except brown butter, into a pot and cover with a lid. Place into a 300-degree oven. Check after 1 hour, then every 30 minutes. Meat is done when a sharp knife goes through with no effort. Remove jowl to wire rack and cool for 30 minutes. Scrape away fat on top and bottom until left with just meat. Slice jowl and place into a pan with brown butter; keep warm. You can brown butter by heating past melting pot; this creates a nutty aroma.

SERVING SUGGESTION:

This luxurious dish is enhanced with a Fireside Manhattan, HANDCRAFTED COCKTAIL section. For Beano's Cabin's hominy recipe, visit www.skitownlife.com

GRILLED ORGANIC EGG

3 Eagle Springs Organic eggs

Preheat grill (using charcoal or pecan/hickory wood chips). Place a perforated grate on the grill and heat for about 10 minutes. Spray grate with pan spray. Crack eggs carefully atop grate and cook for about 3 minutes. Use a spatula and carefully scrape them from the grate.

LAMB SLIDERS
with Pickled Onion Marmalade

SKI TIP • KEYSTONE, COLORADO

The Ski Tip restaurant offers a rotating four-course dinner experience with thoughtful service. The rave reviews continue with Ski Tip's famed desserts guests can enjoy in a comfortable seat next to the rustic fireplace.

8 lamb shanks

2 quarts chicken stock

1 onion, chopped

1 carrot, chopped

2 stalks celery, chopped

1 bay leaf

3 peppercorns

5 sprigs thyme

2 cups red wine

Cornstarch

Slider buns

SERVES 4 - 8

Sear lamb shanks and place in a large pot; add wine, stock, onion, carrot, celery, bay leaf, peppercorn and thyme sprigs. Cover with a heavy lid and braise in a 300-degree oven for 6 - 7 hours or until tender enough to pull apart with a spoon. Remove from oven and cool in liquid. Remove shanks; strain and reserve liquid in separate pot. Simmer and thicken reserved braising liquid with cornstarch to desired consistency for 30 minutes. Pull meat from lamb shanks and fold into thickened sauce.

PICKLED ONION MARMALADE

7 red onions, thinly sliced

2 cups rice wine vinegar

3 cups water

1 cup sugar

3 whole cloves

1 ½ Tbsp. salt

Put all ingredients in a pot and simmer on low-medium heat without stirring until liquid is almost gone.

SERVING SUGGESTION:
Serve pulled lamb on slider buns with the Pickled Onion Marmalade; enjoy with a Ski Tip Coffee, HANDCRAFTED COCKTAIL section.

SWEET TREATS

OATMEAL CREAM PIE AND POTATO CHIP DELIGHT

GRADY'S BAR • SILVERTON, COLORADO

At Silverton Mountain, a skier will find amazing runs in every direction ... imagine a place where the average total snowfall of over 400 inches exceeds the total number of daily visitors. Silverton Mountain claims "all thrills, no frills," much like this simple, thrilling sweet treat from Grady's Bar.

1 Little Debbie Oatmeal Cream Pie

1 snack size bag Lay's Classic Potato Chips

S E R V E S   1

Place oatmeal cream pie on wood burning stove to warm. Place chips on wood burning stove in a single layer. Let each cook for 3 - 5 minutes. Remove from stovetop – you can open the gooey cream pie and place some warm, crisp chips inside.

SERVING SUGGESTION:
This delightfully tasty snack can be relished alongside The Gut Shot cocktail, HANDCRAFTED COCKTAIL section.

SHEILA'S FAMOUS PIONEER MUD PIE

PIONEER SALOON • CHEF SHEILA WITMER • KETCHUM, IDAHO

The Pioneer Saloon is typical of an earlier Idaho where ore wagons rattled down Main Street and business was done with a handshake and a drink. Natural woods, mounted game, and period firearms help recreate an authentic saloon atmosphere at the Pioneer Saloon.

20 Oreo cookies

5 Tbsp. butter, melted

1 tsp. cinnamon

5 pints coffee ice cream, softened

Fudge sauce, thick

Whipped cream

Slivered almonds

SERVES 10 - 12

SERVING SUGGESTION:
Dress the slices of pie with whipped cream and slivered almonds, if desired. Enjoy this dessert with a Hot Toddy cocktail, HANDCRAFTED COCKTAIL section.

MORE DIFFICULT

Process Oreo cookies, butter and cinnamon in a food processor until a fine crumb texture. Press firmly and evenly into bottom and up the sides of a 9-inch spring form pan. The bottom of a glass helps smooth and press up sides. Fill crust with coffee ice cream, up to within ½-inch of top. Make sure crust and ice cream are at the same level. Freeze at least 8 hours or overnight.

Using a spatula, spread fudge sauce on top and then return to the freezer until firm, 2 hours or more. Remove pie from spring form pan. Keep in freezer until ready to serve. Running a sharp knife under hot water is helpful to cleanly slice pie.

BEST EVER CHOCOLATE CHIPPERS

BEAVER CREEK RESORT • AVON, COLORADO

Each year, Beaver Creek hosts a World's Best Chocolate Chip Cookie Competition, as the enjoyment of freshly baked, warm cookies is one of Beaver Creek's most memorable traditions. Throughout October, participants submit cookies and five finalists are chosen to bake 1,000 cookies for the Chocolate Chip Cookie Competition. On opening day, 5,000 cookies are distributed and hungry skiers and riders vote for a favorite. Every afternoon at 3:00, during winter ski season and summer months, a sweet aroma sweeps through Beaver Creek Village. Nearly 500,000 cookies are served each season by chefs with heaped trays of warm, fresh-baked chocolate chip cookies to skiers and snowboarders at the foot of the slopes and throughout the Beaver Creek Village. The Best Ever Chocolate Chippers is courtesy of 2013-2014 Cookie Competition Winner, Nancy Johnson.

1 cup unsalted butter, softened

¾ cup dark brown sugar

½ cup white sugar

1 tsp. vanilla

1 egg

1 tsp. baking soda

2 cups flour

1 ½ cups milk chocolate chips

SERVES 8 - 10

EASIEST

Preheat oven to 350 degrees. Combine flour, soda and salt. Set aside. Beat butter, dark and white sugar, and vanilla until creamy and light-colored, approximately 5 minutes. Beat in egg for another minute. Gradually add flour mixture and mix well. Add chocolate chips until evenly distributed. Bake for 8 - 10 minutes, until slightly golden.

SERVING SUGGESTION:
These cookies are best served warm.

CHOCOLATE DECADENCE

ECHO LAKE INN • CHEF KEVIN BARNES • LUDLOW, VERMONT

After graduating from Johnson and Wales Culinary School and working for two prestigious hotel chains, Chef Kevin realized his true vocation – cooking at a country inn. With Echo Lake Inn, Chef Barnes has been featured in numerous magazines including Gourmet, Bon Appetit, Vermont Magazine, Okemo Magazine *and published in many travel books and newspapers, as well as having one of his recipes promoted in the "Taste of Vermont" campaign.*

6 eggs

3 cups sugar

1 ½ cups butter, melted

1 ½ cups flour

1 cup cocoa

½ tsp. salt

1 Tbsp. vanilla

SERVES 8

Preheat oven to 350 degrees. In a large mixing bowl, combine all ingredients and mix well with a rubber spatula. Do not over-mix. Spray 2 pie plates and divide batter evenly. Cook at 350 degrees for 30 minutes or until done.

SERVING SUGGESTION:
Serve this rich, creamy, chocolate dessert with whipped cream or vanilla ice cream.

KAISERSCHMARRN

PEPI'S RESTAURANT & BAR • CHEF HELMUT KASCHITZ • VAIL, COLORADO

Pepi's Restaurant & Bar showcase continental and American cuisine and specialize in Austrian dishes. These European delicacies resonate with Lindsey Vonn because of her international travel and skiing experiences. Kaiserschmarrn, one of her favorite dishes for après skiing, is an absolute staple in Viennese cuisine and is not only served as dessert, but as a main course.

2 Tbsp. raisins

Dash of rum

6 eggs

1 ½ - 1 ¾ cups milk

Lemon zest, grated

½ Tbsp. vanilla sugar

¾ cup finely ground flour

3 Tbsp. crystal sugar

Pinch of salt

3 ⅓ Tbsp. butter, for frying

1 Tbsp. butter shavings

1 Tbsp. crystal sugar

Powdered sugar and cinnamon

SERVES 4

EASIEST

In a bowl, mix raisins with rum and macerate for 15 minutes. Separate egg whites and yolks, reserving whites and placing yolks in a mixing bowl. Mix milk and yolks, flavor with grated lemon zest and vanilla sugar; add flour. Mix to form a smooth dough.

Beat egg whites together with crystal sugar and a small pinch of salt until it forms a firm peak. Fold egg white mixture into dough. In a 350-degree oven, melt butter in a oven-safe dish or pan, pour in dough mixture and cook for 1 – 2 minutes. Then, sprinkle soaked raisins over the top. Cook until underside is light brown and flip with a spatula. Bake for 6 – 8 minutes until golden brown. Using 2 forks, tear pastry into small pieces. Sprinkle butter shavings over the top, add crystal sugar, and caramelize under a high-heat broiler. Remove from oven, arrange on heated plates and top with powdered sugar and cinnamon.

SERVING SUGGESTION:
Serve with any fruit compote.

HANDCRAFTED COCKTAILS

HEAVENLY MOUNTAIN MARY

UNBUCKLE AT TAMARACK • SOUTH LAKE TAHOE, CALIFORNIA

2 cans V8 juice (46 oz. each)

2 Tbsp. horseradish

1 Tbsp. granulated garlic

1 Tbsp. black pepper

2 Tbsp. dried dill

1 Tbsp. Old Bay seasoning

1 Tbsp. granulated onion

1 Tbsp. celery salt

10 dashes Cholula

½ cup Worcestershire sauce

½ cup pepperoncini juice

4 lemons, juiced

YIELDS 1 GALLON, 8 SERVINGS

To create Mountain Mary Mix, place 1 can V8 and all other ingredients in a blender. Blend for 1 minute on high speed. Then, pour contents of blender into a 1-gallon container and pour the other can of V8 into the container. Refrigerate overnight.

In a pint glass rimmed with salt, fill with ice. Pour in 2 oz. premium vodka and fill glass with Mountain Mary Mix.

SERVING SUGGESTION:
Garnish the cocktail with a skewer of a pickled green beans, pepperoncini, olive, cocktail onion, lemon wedge and lime wedge.

DUSTY'S LEGENDARY CAESAR

DUSTY'S BAR AND BBQ • WHISTLER, BRITISH COLUMBIA

Introduced in 2004, "The Dusty's Caesar" was an instant hit with guests. Since then, Dusty's has sold over 215,000 and has added 5 variations with unique flavor profiles and rims to the menu. Topped with garnishes ranging from pepperoni sticks to beef brisket cubes, this cocktail will excite!

1 oz. Smirnoff Vodka

Clamato juice, to taste

Hot sauce, to taste

Worcestershire sauce, to taste

Mix together first two ingredients; season with hot sauce and Worcestershire sauce.

SERVING SUGGESTION:
Garnish with local Black Tusk beef jerky, a celery stalk and a lime wedge in a celery salt-rimmed glass.

JORDAN BLOODY MARY

SLIDERS RESTAURANT • NEWRY, MAINE

¼ tsp. fresh garlic, peeled whole cloves

3 cups tomato juice

1 Tbsp. horseradish

¼ tsp. celery salt

1 tsp. Cholula hot sauce

1 Tbsp. Sriracha hot sauce

1 tsp. fresh lime juice

1 tsp. fresh lemon juice

1 Tbsp. Peppadew sweet chili peppers, puréed

1 tsp. olive juice

1 tsp. pickle juice

½ tsp. ground smoked black peppercorns

2 dashes Worcestershire sauce

1 ½ oz. bacon-infused Twenty 2 Vodka

MOST DIFFICULT

To create the Jordan Bloody Mix, combine first 12 ingredients into a blender and blend. Pour vodka into pint glass over ice, add bloody mix and shake to combine.

SERVING SUGGESTION:
Garnish with a strip of bacon, some Peppadews and a pickle spear.

WYOMATOE BLOODY MARY

FOUR SEASONS ASCENT LOUNGE • JACKSON HOLE, WYOMING

3 oz. Wyomatoes (Wyoming-grown tomatoes), pureed

1 oz. potato vodka

1 dash Worcestershire sauce

½ oz. lemon juice

1 pinch salt

1 pinch pepper

1 stalk celery

MORE DIFFICULT

Incorporate all ingredients together.

SERVING SUGGESTION:
You may salt the rim of your glass and garnish the drink with a pickled vegetable of your choice.

MOODY'S BLOODY MARY

MOODY'S BISTRO, BAR & BEATS • TRUCKEE, CALIFORNIA

1 ½ oz. vodka of your choice

1 tsp. horseradish

1 Tbsp. Worcestershire sauce

Tabasco to taste

3 turns cracked black pepper

Dash salt

½ lemon, juiced

Tomato juice

EASIEST

Incorporate and shake together all ingredients. Pour into a glass rimmed with celery salt.

SERVING SUGGESTION:
Garnish with a stalk of celery and a lemon wedge.

BLOODY MARY

MT. HOOD MEADOWS • MT. HOOD, OREGON

Bloody Mary Mix

750 ml Monopolowa Vodka

3 Tbsp. fresh basil leaves

1 Tbsp. fresh oregano

4 whole garlic cloves, peeled

 MORE DIFFICULT

Steep for 5 days and strain through coffee filter (enough vodka to make approximately 16 drinks).

Fill a 15 oz. glass completely full of ice and pour 1 ¼ oz. Bloody Mary Vodka and 8 oz. Bloody Mary Mix.

SERVING SUGGESTION:
Garnish with a stalk of celery, a stalk of pickled asparagus, one pepperoncini, one stuffed olive, one slice of lemon and one slice of lime.

BLOODY MARY MIX

7 oz. tomato juice

½ tsp. Dimitri's Seasoning

¼ - ½ tsp. horseradish, pure and uncut

⅓ oz. Sweet 'n Sour

Incorporate all ingredients together.

GREY GOOSE LEMON CITRON BLOODY MARY

OKEMO MOUNTAIN RESORT • LUDLOW, VERMONT

For Okemo Mountain Resort, this is a #1 selling cocktail after the sweet turns and tumbles on the mountain! This is also their propriety tomato mix, which is blended with heirloom Meyer lemon juice and fresh herbs.

2 oz. vodka

6 oz. Bloody Mary Mix

Ice

Optional vegetables: 2 olives, 2 pepperoncini, 2 cherry tomatoes, 2 Meyer lemon slices, 1 green onion stalk and parsley

SERVING SUGGESTION:
Garnish with optional vegetables.

MOST DIFFICULT

Pour vodka and Bloody Mary Mix into a shaker and shake well. Pour over ice.

BLOODY MARY MIX

32 oz. V-8 juice

¼ cup horseradish

3 Tbsp. Worcestershire sauce

2 tsp. celery salt

2 tsp. dill weed

¼ cup pepperoncini juice

4 Tbsp. Meyer lemon juice

4 Tbsp. key lime juice

4 Tbsp. Cara Cara orange juice

3 dashes Tabasco sauce

Place all ingredients in a large container and mix well. Marinate for 24 hours.

MONARCH MOUNTAIN

BLOODY MARY

SIDEWINDER SALOON AT MONARCH MOUNTAIN • MONARCH, COLORADO

3 garlic cloves, peeled

1 onion, halved

2 lemons, sliced

2 limes, sliced

6 jalapenos, sliced

8 habanero peppers

1 red bell pepper, sliced

Vodka

MORE DIFFICULT

To create spicy-infused vodka, add all ingredients to a glass jar, layering each ingredient. A jar with a spigot works best. Fill with vodka and let rest for 4 days or until desired spiciness has been attained. When using a jar with a spigot, place marbles in the bottom of the jar before adding fruit and vegetables. This acts as a filter to prevent clogging. Fill a pint glass with ice. Add 1 shot spicy-infused vodka and fill with Bloody Mary Mix. Garnish with celery stalk, pickle spear, 3 olives, a slice of lemon and a slice of lime.

BLOODY MARY MIX

1 cup Worcestershire sauce

2 Tbsp. celery salt, heaping

4 Tbsp. black pepper

13 shakes Tabasco sauce

1 gallon tomato juice

Mix all ingredients in a gallon container.

7452 MARY

THE ST. REGIS DEER VALLEY • PARK CITY, UTAH

In 1934, Fernand Petiot, the bartender at The St. Regis New York's King Cole Bar, perfected the recipe for a vodka-and-tomato juice cocktail he dubbed the "Bloody Mary." Deemed too racy a name for the hotel's clientele, it was rechristened the Red Snapper. While the latter moniker may not have stood the test of time, Fernand's spicy concoction certainly has. Today, the Bloody Mary remains the signature cocktail of the St. Regis brand, with each hotel crafting its own interpretation of the libation. Elevated like the mountains surrounding The St. Regis Deer Valley, the 7452 Mary features locally-distilled vodka topped with cloud-like celery foam.

1 oz. Vodka 7000' (High West Distillery)

1 dash lemon juice

2 oz. tomato juice

2 pinches black pepper

2 pinches celery salt

3 dashes Worcestershire sauce

2 pinches cayenne pepper

MOST DIFFICULT

Mix together for the 7452 Mary base.

Invert a stemless chardonnay wineglass onto a saucer with simple syrup to coat the rim of the glass. Dip the rim of the glass into black lava salt to coat. Add ice to the prepared glass (be careful not to disturb the black lava salt rim). Pour 7452 Mary base over ice into the prepared stemless chardonnay wineglass; top with celery foam.

CELERY FOAM

48 oz. celery juice

24 oz. green apple juice

3 Tbsp. wasabi powder

1 Tbsp. salt

2 tsp. Xantana

3 limes, juiced

1 parsley bunch, leaves picked

Blend together ingredients and finely strain. Pour foam into a cream-whipper equipped with N_2O cartridge.

SERVING SUGGESTION:
Sprinkle with a dash of cayenne pepper and enjoy.

GINGER JOY

FORKLIFT RESTAURANT • SNOWBIRD, UTAH

1 ¼ oz. Grey Goose La Poire Vodka

¾ oz. Domaine de Canton Ginger Liqueur

Splash fresh lemon juice

Splash simple syrup

Pour ingredients over ice and shake.

SERVING SUGGESTION:
Serve in a martini glass with a slice of lemon.

BASIL GIN DROP

TWIST • BRECKENRIDGE, COLORADO

3 oz. gin of your choice

Heavy splash fresh lemon juice

2 tsp. Ginger Basil Simple Syrup, or to your taste

Fill a shaker with ice and add all ingredients. Shake and strain into a martini glass.

SERVING SUGGESTION:
Garnish with a fresh basil leaf.

GINGER BASIL SIMPLE SYRUP

2 cups water

¼ cup fresh ginger, thinly sliced

Handful fresh basil

½ cup sugar

Heat water in a small saucepan. Add ginger and simmer for 5 minutes, then add basil and simmer for 5 minutes more. Mix in sugar and stir constantly for 5 - 10 minutes. Be careful that the sugar does not burn. Remove from heat and strain. Allow the syrup to cool before adding to the cocktail.

GINGER-TINI

CHARLIE B'S AT STOWEFLAKE • STOWE, VERMONT

1 oz. ginger liquor

¼ oz. lemon juice

1 ½ oz. Green Mountain Distillers Lemon Vodka

Splash Cold Hollow Cider

Mix together all ingredients and shake.

SERVING SUGGESTION:
Serve up or on the rocks with fresh ginger.

MAD RIVER GLEN

STARK & STORMY

GENERAL STARK'S PUB • WAITSFIELD, VERMONT

1 - 2 oz. Sailor Jerry's spiced rum

Rookie's ginger beer

Fresh lime

Fill a 10 – 12 oz. cocktail glass with ice. Mix together rum, ginger beer and a fresh lime.

SERVING SUGGESTION:
Enjoy this tongue-in-cheek cocktail, as a word play on General Stark's Pub, where it is served.

MOONSTRUCK MULE

CAMP AT GRAND SUMMIT HOTEL • NEWRY, MAINE

2 oz. Cold River Blueberry Vodka

⅛ oz. fresh lime juice

6 oz. Gosling's ginger beer

EASIEST

In a 12 oz. pint glass filled with ice, combine all ingredients.

SERVING SUGGESTION: Garnish this cocktail with Maine blueberries.

NORTHSTAR

SIERRA SUNSET

THE BACKYARD BAR AND BBQ AND THE LIVING ROOM AT RITZ CARLTON • TRUCKEE, CALIFORNIA

1 ½ oz. Makers Mark

¼ oz. lemon juice

4 dashes Angostura bitters

Ginger beer

EASIEST

Combine first three ingredients in a shaker with ice. Shake rigorously and double-strain in a glass with fresh ice. Fill and top-off with a ginger beer of your choice.

SERVING SUGGESTION: Garnish with a lemon wheel.

SERVING SUGGESTION:
Garnish with a rosemary sprig, an apple chip and a pear chip.

COCKTAIL #18

LAUNDRY KITCHEN & COCKTAILS • MIXOLOGIST TOD (JJ) JOHNSON • STEAMBOAT SPRINGS, COLORADO

A spin on one of Laundry's long running cocktails (in their list of several hundred), Cocktail #18 is classically winter in spirit. As one can see, Laundry has the same "hand crafted" approach to the beverage program that they have to their scratch kitchen – crafting shrubs (drinking vinegars), simple syrups and infused spirits.

1 ½ oz. Pear-Apple Infused Vodka

½ oz. Pear-Fennel Shrub

½ oz. Rosemary Simple Syrup

2 oz. ginger beer

 MOST DIFFICULT

For a single serving, shake and pour first 3 ingredients over ice, then top with ginger beer.

ROSEMARY SIMPLE SYRUP

1 cup sugar

1 ½ cups water

2 rosemary sprigs

Boil water and 1 cup of sugar, then cool. Add 2 rosemary sprigs. Infuse in the refrigerator for 1 week, then strain through fine filter.

APPLE AND PEAR CHIPS

1 Gala apple

1 pear

Core 1 apple and 1 pear, then cut into very thin slices. Place in a dehydrator for recommended time according to manufacturer (can be placed in oven at 500 degrees until chip size, if no dehydrator is available).

PEAR-FENNEL SHRUB

1 pear

1 cup sugar

1 Tbsp. crushed fennel seeds

1 cup champagne vinegar

½ pinch salt

To create this drinking vinegar, core and cube pear then combine with sugar and fennel seeds in a glass bowl. Stir to gently break up the fruit. Cover with plastic wrap and refrigerate for 24 hours. Stir in champagne vinegar and salt, cover and return to refrigerator for 1 week. Pour through a fine strainer while gently pressing the fruit to release all juices. Refrigerate for one more week before using.

PEAR-APPLE INFUSED VODKA

1 liter vodka

2 Gala apples

2 pears

1 tsp. maple syrup

Pinch cinnamon

Pinch allspice

Core 2 apples and 2 pears, then cut into wedges. Toss wedges in a bowl with maple syrup, cinnamon and allspice. Roast at 400 degrees for fifteen minutes.

Add the roasted fruit to the vodka and infuse for 1 - 2 weeks.

THE IMPERIALIST

TERRA BISTRO • MIXOLOGIST BEN WANNER • VAIL, COLORADO

2 oz. Ron Zacapa Rum

½ oz. Green Chartreuse

Ginger People ginger beer

Mix together first two ingredients in a tall glass. Top with ginger beer, preferably Ginger People, as it's organic with a strong ginger flavor.

SERVING SUGGESTION:
Garnish the cocktail with a lime wedge.

ASPEN MOUNTAIN

DROP THE BEET

AJAX TAVERN AT THE LITTLE NELL • ASPEN, COLORADO

½ oz. beet vodka

2 oz. Domaine de Canton

½ oz. each of lemon, lime and orange juice

Mix all ingredients in a shaker until well blended, pour into a raw/white sugar-rimmed martini glass.

SERVING SUGGESTION:
Garnish with an orange slice.

THE GEOFFERY

THE FARM • PARK CITY, UTAH

1 ½ oz. Old Tom's Ransom Gin

½ oz. Campari

¼ oz. lemon juice

¼ oz. Ginger Shrub - specific sweet-and-sour ginger syrup

EASIEST

Shake together all ingredients.

SERVING SUGGESTION:
Serve up with a lemon peel.

SNOWMASS

MOSCOW MONK

LYNN BRITT CABIN • SNOWMASS, COLORADO

1 ½ oz. Woody Creek Vodka

½ oz. Chartreuse

1 oz. lime juice

½ oz. simple syrup

Ginger beer

EASIEST

Mix together first four ingredients, then top with ginger beer.

SERVING SUGGESTION:
Garnish cocktail with a thyme sprig.

LA COSA NOSTRA

TERRA BISTRO • MIXOLOGIST BEN WANNER • VAIL, COLORADO

2 oz. Herradura silver tequila

1 oz. Solerno blood orange liqueur

½ oz. simple syrup

½ oz. lemon juice

½ oz. blood orange juice

Shake together all ingredients. Pour into a glass of your choice.

SERVING SUGGESTION:
Serve up with a flamed orange twist.

GRASS SKIRT

TERRA BISTRO • MIXOLOGIST BEN WANNER • VAIL, COLORADO

2 oz. Barsol Pisco

½ oz. lime juice

½ oz. simple syrup

3 pieces pineapple, muddled

½ oz. Velvet Falernum

Shake together all ingredients. Pour the cocktail into a tall glass over ice.

SERVING SUGGESTION:
Top the libation with coconut milk foam.

COSMOPOLITAN

THE COTTAGE AT MIRROR LAKE INN • LAKE PLACID, NEW YORK

2 oz. P3 Placid Vodka

½ oz. Triple Sec

Dash fresh lime juice

Dash cranberry juice

In a shaker filled with ice, add all ingredients. Shake hard and strain into a chilled martini glass.

SERVING SUGGESTION:
Garnish with a fresh wedge of lime.

SCHWEITZER MOUNTAIN RESORT

ICY COCONUT COSMO

CHIMNEY ROCK GRILLE • SANDPOINT, IDAHO

2 oz. Malibu Rum

3 lime wedges, juiced

Dash cranberry juice

Sprite

Add first three ingredients to a cocktail mixer glass with ice, and shake. Pour into rocks glass filled with ice and top off with a splash of Sprite.

SERVING SUGGESTION:
Garnish with a lemon wedge, lime wedge and a cherry.

SPICY PEACH LEMON DROP

THE BLACKSMITH RESTAURANT • BEND, OREGON

2 slices fresh jalapenos

2 oz. 360 Georgia Peach Vodka

3 dashes peach bitters

2 oz. organic peach nectar

1 oz. fresh lemon juice

1 oz. simple syrup

Muddle jalapenos. Shake together all ingredients.

SERVING SUGGESTION:
Strain into a sugar-rimmed martini glass. Serve up with a lemon wedge.

CRESTED BUTTE CRUSH

THE LAST STEEP • CRESTED BUTTE, COLORADO

1 oz. Stoli Orange

1 oz. Stoli Vanilla

1 oz. Southern Comfort

Fanta Orange Soda

Dash of cream or half-and-half

Incorporate all ingredients in a mixer and shake well.

SERVING SUGGESTION:
Garnish with a Maraschino cherry or two.

PERFECT RASPBERRY LEMONADE COCKTAIL

JJ'S ROCKY MOUNTAIN TAVERN • COPPER MOUNTAIN, COLORADO

6 oz. Fresh-Squeezed Lemonade

1 oz. Barenjager Honey & Pear Liqueur

1 oz. Raspberry Liqueur

 Create the cocktail by incorporating lemonade with liqueurs.

FRESH-SQUEEZED LEMONADE

1 cup water

1 cup sugar

1 cup lemon juice, freshly squeezed

3 - 4 cups cold water

To create bartender Paulie Werner's Fresh-Squeezed Lemonade, heat 1 cup water and sugar in a small sauce pan until sugar completely dissolves. Pour this into a pitcher; add the lemon juice and enough cold water to dilute to desired strength.

SERVING SUGGESTION:
Serve the cocktail over ice and garnish with slices of fresh lemon.

RASPBERRY ROYALE COCKTAIL

CB (COVERED BRIDGE) GRILLE • COPPER MOUNTAIN, COLORADO

1 ½ oz. Svedka Citron Vodka

½ oz. Black Raspberry Liqueur

5 whole raspberries

3 basil leaves

Splash Prosecco

1 lemon peel

 CB Grille bartender, Kayla Alaimo, recommends muddling the fruit, straining it and then muddling it again with the basil. Add the muddled ingredients to an ice-filled glass. Pour vodka and liqueur into glass. Top with Prosecco.

SERVING SUGGESTION:
Use fresh raspberries for garnish.

STRAWBERRY-BASIL PRESS

THE 10TH • VAIL, COLORADO

2 basil leaves

2 strawberries

1 lemon wedge

1 lime wedge

1 ½ oz. Strawberry-Lemonade Svedka vodka

½ oz. agave nectar

Club soda

MORE DIFFICULT

Muddle first four ingredients together with ice. Add vodka and nectar and shake well. Strain the cocktail into a double old-fashioned glass with fresh ice. Top with club soda.

SERVING SUGGESTION:

Garnish the drink with a basil leaf and a strawberry.

ARANCIATA ROSSA LEMON FIZZ

TALISKER CLUB • PARK CITY, UTAH

2 oz. Vodka 7000' (High West Distillery)

3 oz. San Pellegrino Limonata sparkling water

2 oz. San Pellegrino Aranciata Rossa sparkling water

½ small blood orange, juiced

Chef Roger Laws recommends filling a glass with crushed ice, squeezing in blood orange juice while straining seeds and adding vodka, limonata and aranciata sparkling water.

SERVING SUGGESTION:
Garnish with a Meyer lemon wedge and a blood orange wedge.

SUGARBUSH RESORT

CLOCKWORK ORANGE

TIMBERS RESTAURANT • WAITSFIELD, VERMONT

1 ½ oz. Stoli Orange

1 oz. Lillet Blanc

1 ½ oz. grapefruit juice

½ tsp. honey

Dash orange bitters

Combine all ingredients for a single serving and serve over ice.

SQUAW VALLEY

LOCAL'S LEMONADE

KT BASE BAR • OLYMPIC VALLEY, CALIFORNIA

1 ½ oz. Titos Vodka

½ oz. St. Germain (elderflower liquor)

½ lemon, juiced

Soda water

Combine first three ingredients and top with desired amount of soda water for a single serving.

SERVING SUGGESTION:
Serve over ice.

MT. HOOD SKI BOWL

LIME-AID

SKAMANIA LODGE • CHEF MARK HENRY • STEVENSON, WASHINGTON

4 slices cucumber, muddled

½ lime, juiced

1 ½ oz. Uncle Vals Botanical Gin

½ oz. simple syrup

Club soda

EASIEST

Muddle sliced cucumbers in pint glass or cocktail shaker. Add lime juice, gin and simple syrup. Cover and mix vigorously for 15 seconds. Strain into a glass with ice and top off with soda.

SERVING SUGGESTION:
Garnish with an extra slice of cucumber and a lime wedge.

ELIXIR 16

FROST BAR AT THE SEBASTIAN HOTEL • VAIL, COLORADO

Seasonal fruit of your choice

½ oz. St. Germain Liquor

La Marca Prosecco

In a white wine glass, fill halfway with ice and fresh, seasonal fruit. Add St. Germain and top-off with Prosecco.

SERVING SUGGESTION:
Enjoy unadorned!

ITALIAN CREAM SODA

EATS OF EDEN • EDEN, UTAH

1 Tbsp. strawberry flavored drink syrup (or other favorite flavor)

1 Tbsp. heavy cream

½ cup 7-Up, Sprite or other lemon lime soda

¾ cup ice

1 oz. white rum

Whipped cream

Maraschino cherries

In a 9 – 12 oz. glass, add syrup and rum. Add soda, ice and cream. Garnish with whipped cream and cherries. Omit rum for a mocktail.

SERVING SUGGESTION:

Serving with a cocktail straw to mix cream before drinking makes a fun presentation. You can also mix the cream into the drink before serving, for a creamy look.

VAIL MOUNTAIN

THE ANTI-OXIDANT

FROST BAR AT THE SEBASTIAN HOTEL • VAIL, COLORADO

2 oz. berry-infused vodka

½ oz. pomegranate liqueur

¼ oz. cranberry juice

¼ oz. simple syrup

¼ oz. lime juice

To make berry-infused vodka, simply add muddled, fresh, ripe, in-season berries to Belvedere Vodka (or another brand of your choice). Soak overnight. Recommended berries: raspberries, strawberries and blueberries.

Incorporate all ingredients with ice and shake well. For this single serving, strain the liquid into a martini glass.

SERVING SUGGESTION:

Garnish with fresh whole berries.

THE CAMPFIRE

KANU LOUNGE • LAKE PLACID, NEW YORK

Bartender Zachary Blair created this drink, which is inspired by Whiteface Lodge's natural surroundings. It brings together the aromas and flavors synonymous with the Adirondack region. The combination of brown spirits create a hearty, wholesome drink ideal for outdoor enthusiasts. The sage leaves embody the smell of the underbrush and forests in the Adirondack Park and the scotch is reminiscent of the carnal smell of burning campfires.

2 oz. Buffalo Trace Bourbon

½ oz. maple water (half maple syrup, half water)

1 lemon wedge, juiced

Rolfs Cider

Compass Box "Peat Monster" Scotch

2 sage leaves, torn

Grilled apple and sage leaf for garnish

 MORE DIFFICULT

Fill a highball glass with ice, and add bourbon, maple water, squeezed lemon wedge. Top with cider. Roughly tear two sage leaves and add to the drink. Toss the ingredients in a mixing glass. Float a splash of peaty scotch on top.

SERVING SUGGESTION:
Garnish with a grilled apple ring and sage leaf.

EVERYTHING BUT THE WORM

KANU LOUNGE • LAKE PLACID, NEW YORK

The Del Maguey hand-bottled, organic mezcal carries a warm, rich taste, accented with a subtle smokiness; this supports the richness of the Kanu Lounge Chili con Carne, the pairing suggestion. The sweetness of the pineapple brings viscosity to the drink and plays off the spiciness of the chili. The cilantro adds a fresh, green, herbal note, tying in the taste of the chili. Zachary Blair, bartender at Kanu Lounge, states that the components of the drink act as an aromatic and flavorful palate cleanser.

2 oz. Del Maguey "Minero," Single Village Mezcal

1 ½ oz. tamarind juice

1 oz. pineapple juice

Splash lemon juice

1 oz. Lake Placid Pub and Brewery's IPA

Fresh cilantro

 MORE DIFFICULT

In a highball glass, combine all ingredients over ice. Add a few torn leaves of cilantro to increase the aromatic qualities. Shake the drink a couple times between another highball glass to incorporate.

SERVING SUGGESTION:
Garnish with a sprig of cilantro.

SILVER FORK LODGE'S BARTENDER'S MARGARITA

SILVER FORK LODGE • BRIGHTON, UTAH

1 oz. Patron tequila

Sweet and Sour Mix

Sweetened lime juice

1 oz. Grand Marnier

Add salt to the top of a margarita glass (optional) and fill with ice. Add tequila and fill the glass ⅔ full with sweet and sour mix. Continue to fill the glass almost to the top with sweetened lime juice and finish with Grand Marnier.

SERVING SUGGESTION:
Garnish the cocktail with a lime wedge.

MAYAHUELA'S MARGARITA

LARKSPUR RESTAURANT • VAIL, COLORADO

According to ancient Aztec lore, Mayahuel was the goddess of the agave plant and is credited with discovering the process of distilling agave into tequila. This new twist on the classic margarita was inspired by Larkspur's mixologist's regular trips to Mexico when the snows in Vail recede. It pays homage to the Aztec tradition of creating the most unique and compelling liquors from the mystical blue plant.

1 slice cucumber, ¼-inch thick

2 oz. Herradura Reposado Tequila

1 ¼ oz. blue agave simple syrup

1 oz. lime juice

¼ oz. red pepper juice, approximately 4 drops

In a martini shaker, muddle cucumber. Add tequila, agave, lime juice and red pepper juice. Shake with ice.

SERVING SUGGESTION:
Serve up in a chilled martini glass.

BOGART'S FAMOUS MARGARITA

BOGART'S RESTAURANT • RED LODGE, MONTANA

Established in 1975, Bogart's is a destination restaurant for locals and out of town guests alike. At Bogart's, a fun staff and unique atmosphere are combined with seriously good Mexican food and legendary margaritas to provide guests with an unforgettable dining experience in Red Lodge. No matter which Mexican entrée you choose, it will be a fiesta to your taste buds, much like Bogart's Famous Margarita recipe.

1 ½ oz. Jose Cuervo Gold Tequila

¾ oz. Bols Triple Sec

Sweet and sour mix

Fill a large glass with ice, add 2 liquors and Bogart's bartender, Reanna Fey, suggests balancing the drink with your favorite sweet and sour mix. Shake well. Salt the rim of your margarita glass with kosher salt, if desired.

SERVING SUGGESTION:
Serve with a freshly squeezed lime wheel.

WILD & SPICY MARGARITA

DOUBLE BLACK NOODLE BAR AT WILDWOOD SNOWMASS • SNOWMASS VILLAGE, COLORADO

1 ½ oz. Don Julio Tequila

½ oz. Cointreau

½ oz. Agave

¼ tsp. Serrano peppers, chopped

2 - 3 sprigs cilantro

2 oz. fresh lime juice

Splash soda water

Muddle Serrano pepper and cilantro. Add tequila, Cointreau and agave, then add fresh lime juice. Top with a splash of soda water.

SERVING SUGGESTION:
Serve on ice in a salt-rimmed glass. Garnish with a lime wedge and cilantro sprig.

BARTENDER'S MARGARITA

THE SILVER DOLLAR BAR AND GRILL AT THE WORT HOTEL • JACKSON, WYOMING

1 ¾ oz. Jose Cuervo tequila

½ oz. Patron Citronage

4 oz. Sweet and sour mix

½ oz. Grand Marnier

Bartender Mike Reisbeck suggests preparing a pint glass with ice and a salted rim. To the glass, add tequila, Patron and sweet and sour mix. Top off with Grand Marnier.

SERVING SUGGESTION:
Serve with a freshly squeezed lime.

HUCKLEBERRY MARTINI (HUCKLETINI)

BRANDING IRON GRILL • ALTA, WYOMING

1 ½ oz. 44 North Vodka or Huckleberry Vodka

½ oz. Cointreau or Triple Sec

Fresh lime juice

Fresh huckleberries with simple syrup

Add a teaspoon of whole huckleberries to bottom of martini glass. In a pint glass, muddle lime juice and huckleberries with syrup. Fill the glass with ice and add huckleberry vodka and Cointreau. Shake and strain into prepared martini glass.

TAMARACK RESORT

I'M YOUR HUCKLEBERRY MARTINI

MORELS & DELISH CATERING • TAMARACK, IDAHO

¼ - ½ cup huckleberries, fresh or frozen

3 parts 44 North Vodka or Huckleberry Vodka

1 part Cointreau orange liquor

1 part lime juice, freshly squeezed

MORE DIFFICULT

Muddle locally picked huckleberries (the state fruit of Idaho). In an ice-filled shaker, incorporate huckleberries, huckleberry vodka, Cointreau, and lime juice. Mixologist Jan Bittenbender advises to shake well and pour in a chilled martini glass.

SERVING SUGGESTION:
Garnish with lime curl.

YELLOWSTONE CLUB

HUCKLEBERRY LIMEADE

YELLOWSTONE CLUB • BIG SKY, MONTANA

4 oz. white sugar

1 cup fresh lime juice

4 oz. frozen huckleberries

4 oz. Grey Goose Vodka

Fresh mint

Shake together all ingredients; pour into chilled pint glasses filled with ice.

SERVING SUGGESTION:
Serve with fresh mint.

HUCKLEBERRY BRAMBLE

RUPERT'S AT HOTEL MCCALL • MCCALL, IDAHO

Rogue Pink Spruce Gin

Soda water

Sour mix (1 part fresh-squeezed lemon juice, 1 part simple syrup)

Huckleberries

Lemon peel

Shake equal parts of first 3 ingredients with huckleberries and lemon peel together with ice in a cocktail shaker, and then strain into a glass over ice.

SERVING SUGGESTION:
Chris Stewart, bartender of Rupert's, suggests garnishing with huckleberries and a lemon twist.

HUCKLEBERRY LEMONADE

CHET'S BAR AND GRILL • BIG SKY, MONTANA

1 ½ oz. Huckleberry Vodka

Wild Mountain Huckleberries

Lemonade

Mix together all ingredients.

SERVING SUGGESTION:
Garnish with a lemon wedge.

NATIVA TERRA SANGRIA

COPPER CONFERENCE CENTER • COPPER MOUNTAIN, COLORADO

1 bottle (750 ml) Nativa Terra
Cabernet Sauvignon

1 cup light Agave

1 large lemon, sliced

1 large orange, sliced

1 large apple, cut into thin
sections

3 - 4 oz. brandy or Pisco

12 oz. soda water

YIELDS 2 QUARTS

MORE DIFFICULT In a glass pitcher, incorporate wine, Agave and fruit. Let the mixture rest in the refrigerator for 12 - 24 hours. One hour prior to serving, add the brandy and soda water. Serve in chilled wine glasses with or without ice.

SERVING SUGGESTION:
Place macerated fruit into each glass.

WHITE SANGRIA

ROCKER@SQUAW • OLYMPIC VALLEY, CALIFORNIA

1 bottle Pinot Grigio

¼ cup simple syrup (sugar dissolved in
water with 1:1 ratio)

1 whole lemon, freshly squeezed

1 whole orange, freshly squeezed

⅓ cup Triple Sec

8 sprigs fresh rosemary

½ cup pomegranate seeds

½ cup pomegranate juice

SERVES 4 – 6

MORE DIFFICULT Soak ½ the rosemary in the wine, simple syrup, lemon juice, orange juice and triple sec overnight or up to 24 hours. The next day, remove rosemary and discard. Set out 4 glasses and splash the pomegranate juice on the bottom, then fill cups with ice and pour sangria mixture over top.

SERVING SUGGESTION:
Evenly distribute pomegranate seeds and the rest of the rosemary on top,
as a garnish.

SPRING TEASER

KELLY LIKEN • VAIL, COLORADO

1 ½ oz. Breckenridge Bourbon

1 oz. rosemary honey simple syrup

3 Bergamot Tea ice cubes

½ oz. egg white

Dash whiskey barrel bitters

Mix all ingredients together and shake.
Pour cocktail into a Collins glass.

SERVING SUGGESTION:
Garnish this drink with a rosemary sprig.

VAIL MOUNTAIN

GET HI-ON-BISCUS

KELLY LIKEN • VAIL, COLORADO

2 oz. Lemongrass Snova Vodka

1 oz. hibiscus simple syrup

½ oz. ginger liqueur

Dash gin

Orange bitters

Dash lemon juice

Infuse vodka with lemongrass for 24 hours or more.
Then, mix all ingredients together and shake well. Serve
in a martini glass.

SERVING SUGGESTION:
Garnish this cocktail with an edible flower.

THE ALPENGLOW

KELLY LIKEN • VAIL, COLORADO

1 ½ oz. Woody Creek vodka

1 oz. Cocchi Americano

1 ½ oz. grapefruit juice

½ oz. egg white

Dash angostura bitters

Grapefruit zest

MORE DIFFICULT

Combine all ingredients except the grapefruit zest, and mix well. Pour this cocktail in a glass without ice.

SERVING SUGGESTION:
Top cocktail with grapefruit zest.

BURNT MARTINI

FORTY-ONE SOUTH • SAGLE, IDAHO

¼ oz. premium scotch

2 oz. premium vodka

Pour scotch into a martini glass and swirl to coat the glass. Do not pour out the excess. Shake vodka in a martini shaker with ice, until very cold. Strain the vodka into the martini glass.

SERVING SUGGESTION:
Garnish with bleu cheese-stuffed olives.

VERMONT VESPER COCKTAIL

THE DOWNTOWN GROCERY • CHEF ROGAN LECHTHALER • LUDLOW, VERMONT

The specially chosen gin in this cocktail is made with wild Vermont juniper berries. When it is paired with the herbaceous apple wine and either a large twist of orange or slice of a local apple, this cocktail is tremendously fruity and refreshing.

2 oz. Vermont Spirits Coppers Gin

1 oz. Vermont Spirits White Vodka

1 oz. Eden Ice Cider Company's Orleans Herbal

Slice local apple or large orange twist for garnish.

Fill pint glass with ice and measured liquid ingredients. Shake and pour into a chilled martini glass.

SERVING SUGGESTION:
Garnish this cocktail with a local apple slice or large orange twist.

HIGH SPEED COCKTAIL

LONGFELLOW'S RESTAURANT • KINGFIELD, MAINE

This cocktail is named after one crazy night in small-town Kingfield, Maine, where a police chase ended in pursuit of 2 people who raced over the Canadian border. This evening caused commotion and excitement and inspired Canadian bartender, Kristin Wallaker's, popular drink.

1 ½ oz. Captain Morgan's Spiced Rum

Splash Chambord

Pineapple juice

Fill a glass with ice, then add rum, a generous splash of Chambord and top with pineapple juice.

SERVING SUGGESTION:
Garnish this cocktail with a local apple slice or large orange twist.

BULLEIT PROOF

FOUNDRY AT SUMMIT POND • KILLINGTON, VERMONT

2 wedges fresh lemon

½ tsp. granulated sugar

2 oz. Bulleit Frontier Whiskey

Muddle lemon and sugar. Stir in whiskey.

SERVING SUGGESTION:
Serve on the rocks with a lemon peel garnish and, possibly,
a Vermont maple sugar rim.

LITTLE RED JACK WAGON

RIVERHORSE ON MAIN • PARK CITY, UTAH

1 ½ oz. Apple Jack Brandy

½ oz. lime juice

½ oz. grenadine

4 dashes bitters

Club soda

In a rocks glass, add first four ingredients. Top with soda.

SERVING SUGGESTION:
Garnish with lime wheel and
a cherry.

DEER VALLEY RESORT

APRÈS CIDRE

DALY'S PUB AT MONTAGE DEER VALLEY • PARK CITY, UTAH

1 ½ oz. Whitetail caramel whiskey

1 oz. caramel syrup

3 oz. Stella Artois Cidre

In a shaker, combine whiskey and caramel syrup. Shake and strain into a martini glass. Fill the remainder of the glass with Stella Artois Cidre.

SERVING SUGGESTION:
Garnish with a ½ caramel-dipped red apple slice.

BLACK MANHATTAN

STEIN ERIKSEN LODGE • PARK CITY, UTAH

1 ½ oz. Woodford Reserve

½ oz. Fernet Branca

½ oz. Patron XO Café

1 orange wedge, squeezed

2 shakes of bitters

1 egg white

Stir liquors in shaker with spoon. In second shaker with ice, shake orange, bitters, and egg white until foamy. Using a bar spoon to keep separate, strain liquors from first shaker into martini glass and strain foamy mixture on top.

SERVING SUGGESTION:
Garnish top with drops of bitters to make a design of your choice.

ASPEN MOUNTAIN

CHAIR 9 YARD SALE

CHAIR 9 AT THE LITTLE NELL • ASPEN, COLORADO

1 ½ oz. vodka

1 ½ oz. rum

1 ½ oz. tequila

1 ½ oz. gin

1 oz. sour mix (equal parts lemon juice & simple syrup)

Cola of your choice

EASIEST

In a glass filled with ice, combine ingredients and top with cola.

SERVING SUGGESTION:
Garnish with a slice of lemon.

SNOWMASS

FRENCH QUARTER 75

SAGE RESTAURANT • SNOWMASS, COLORADO

2 oz. cognac

½ oz. lemon juice

½ oz. simple syrup

1 oz. Champagne

Combine first three ingredients, then top with Champagne.

SERVING SUGGESTION:
Bartender Brit White recommends garnishing with a lemon twist.

BANDALERO

THE GRILL AT AMANGANI • JACKSON, WYOMING

2 oz. Don Julio Añejo Tequila

½ oz. Cointreau

2 oz. apple cider

¼ lime, juiced

Splash orange juice

½ tsp. chipotle powder

Mesquite-smoked sea salt

Squeeze lime juice into a metal cocktail shaker, then add tequila, Cointreau, apple cider, orange juice and chipotle powder. Add ice and shake vigorously. Strain mixture into an ice-filled glass rimmed with sea salt.

SERVING SUGGESTION:
Suspend a fresh lime wedge on the rim of the glass.

MASON MAPLE SHANDY

HYDE AWAY INN AND RESTAURANT • WAITSFIELD, VERMONT

¾ oz. Vermont maple syrup

2 oz. bourbon

3 oz. lemonade

3 oz. Vermont pilsner draft beer

In a 16 oz. mason jar with ice, combine all ingredients. Shake or stir to incorporate.

SERVING SUGGESTION:
Garnish with lemon wheel.

HANDCRAFTED COCKTAILS 261

ALPEN TWINKLE

CLUB CAR RESTAURANT • WINTER PARK, COLORADO

1 ½ oz. St. Germain liqueur

1 ½ oz. pear vodka

4 oz. Champagne

Super-fine sugar

Mix together first two ingredients, then finish with Champagne in a wine glass rimmed with super-fine sugar.

SERVING SUGGESTION:
Garnish with a lemon twist.

MT BACHELOR

CINNAMON TOAST CRUNCH

BROKEN TOP CLUB • BEND, OREGON

1 ½ oz. Fireball Cinnamon Whisky

1 ½ oz. Orchata Cinnamon Cream Rum

Pour over rocks.

SERVING SUGGESTION:
Garnish with a Maraschino cherry.

KINKY SUE

FORMERLY OF JOHN'S ANGELS CATERING • LAKESIDE, MONTANA

1 ½ oz. Kinky liqueur

1 oz. chilled vodka

2 ½ oz. club soda

Splash pineapple juice

Splash lime juice

EASIEST

Shake all ingredients with ice in a shaker. Pour into a rock or martini glass.

SERVING SUGGESTION:

Bartender Austin Deitrick suggests garnishing the cocktail with a lime wedge.

SUN VALLEY RESORT

ITALIAN KIR ROYALE

ENOTECA • KETCHUM, IDAHO

¼ oz. (approximately 1 Tbsp.) Crème de Cassis

Adami Prosecco

EASIEST

Add Crème de Cassis to a wine or champagne glass; fill the remainder of the glass with Prosecco.

SERVING SUGGESTION:

Garnish with 4 raspberries.

ST. GERMAIN SPRITZ

KETCHUM GRILL • KETCHUM, IDAHO

1 part St. Germain

2 parts Duval Leroy Champagne

Fresh lemon juice

Combine St. Germain and Champagne. Add a squeeze of fresh lemon juice.

SERVING SUGGESTION:

Owner Anne Mason suggests garnishing this cocktail with 2 - 4 fresh blueberries, a large lemon zest and fresh mint.

TELLURIDE SKI RESORT

PURA VIDA

NEW SHERIDAN CHOP HOUSE RESTAURANT • TELLURIDE, COLORADO

3 oz. Vago Mescal

Lime, to taste

Honey, to taste

½ oz. Domain de Canton

Muddled Cucumber

Sal de Gusano

Combine all ingredients in a shaker and mix well. Strain into a glass rimmed with Sal de Gusano, an Oaxacan spice.

SERVING SUGGESTION:

Serve up.

THE PERFECT GENTLEMAN

WESTBANK GRILL AT FOUR SEASONS • JACKSON, WYOMING

2 oz. Makers Mark or other bourbon

½ oz. Drambuie

½ oz. sweet vermouth

2 splashes orange bitters

Fill a shaker with ice and add all ingredients. Shake vigorously. In a chilled martini glass, place a brandied cherry and pour the cocktail over it.

SERVING SUGGESTION:
Finish off the "perfect" cocktail with an orange twist.

ESPRESSO MARTINI

CARBON COUNTY STEAKHOUSE • RED LODGE, MONTANA

2 ¼ oz. Three Olives Espresso Vodka

¾ oz. Frangelico Liqueur

Shake with ice then strain into a chilled martini glass.

SERVING SUGGESTION:
Garnish with a twist of lemon.

ASPEN MOUNTAIN

ALPINE GEM

39 DEGREES AT THE SKY HOTEL • ASPEN, COLORADO

1 ¼ oz. Reyka Vodka

½ oz. Yellow Chartreuse

¼ oz. Kubler Absinthe

2 oz. fresh grapefruit juice

½ oz. simple syrup

3 – 4 drops Peychaud's bitters

Mixologist Denis Cote's wickedly creative cocktails are the perfect match for 39 Degrees' flavorful food. As voted by USA Today, 39 Degrees was recently named one of the Top Nine snug hotel bars to warm you up in winter.

In a mixing glass, add all ingredients. Add ice and stir for 20 seconds. Strain cocktail over a large ice cube in a double old-fashioned glass. Finish with 3 - 4 drops of Peychaud's bitters.

STEAMBOAT RESORT

SPRING INTO THE ROCKIES MARTINI

OLD TOWN PUB • STEAMBOAT SPRINGS, COLORADO

2 oz. top shelf Colorado gin

½ oz. elderflower liqueur

1 slice fresh lemon

Shake together gin, elderflower liqueur and freshly squeezed lemon juice with ice, then strain into a chilled martini glass.

SERVING SUGGESTION:
Garnish with a lemon twist.

TAOS SUNSET

THE BLONDE BEAR TAVERN • TAOS SKI VALLEY, NEW MEXICO

1 ½ oz. premium vodka

4 ½ oz. freshly-squeezed orange juice

1 oz. carrot juice

1 oz. beet juice

Dash red wine vinegar

EASIEST

Combine all ingredients and pour over ice.

SERVING SUGGESTION:
Garnish with an orange slice.

SMUGGLERS' NOTCH RESORT

APRÈS MAIN

158 MAIN • JEFFERSONVILLE, VERMONT

3 ½ oz. Boyden Valley Vermont
Ice Maple Cream Liqueur

2 oz. Smugglers' Notch Distillery
Vodka

Maple Sugar

EASIEST

Dust the rim of a martini glass with maple sugar. Shake first two
ingredients with ice, then pour into prepared glass.

BRUNDAGE MOUNTAIN RESORT

NIGHT SKY OVER PAYETTE LAKE

SHORE LODGE • MCCALL, IDAHO

1 oz. Cascade Mountain Gin

½ oz. elderflower liqueur

½ oz. fresh lemon juice

3 basil leaves

1 star anise

Soda water

1 slice lemon

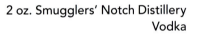

EASIEST

In a mixing glass, add gin, elderflower, lemon juice and basil leaves.
Muddle together, then strain into a glass over fresh ice. Fill with soda
water.

SERVING SUGGESTION:
Garnish with lemon slice and star anise.

THE SKI BREEZE

8100 MOUNTAINSIDE BAR AND GRILL • BARTENDER WENDY HARTNETT • AVON, COLORADO

¾ oz. St. Germaine Elderflower Liquor

¾ oz. simple syrup

½ lemon, juiced

5 mint leaves

1 ½ oz. Citron Vodka

Prosecco

In a mixing glass, combine elderflower liquor, simple syrup lemon and mint leaves. Muddle well. Add vodka and ice, then gently shake 3 times. Pour contents into a highball glass, unstrained. Top with Prosecco.

SERVING SUGGESTION:
Enjoy simply and unadorned.

THE FRONTIER

J-BAR AT HOTEL JEROME • ASPEN, COLORADO

1 ½ oz. Leopold Bros Maryland-Style Rye Whiskey

½ oz. Sercial Madeira

½ oz. fresh squeezed lemon juice

½ oz. simple syrup

Splash of Cointreau

1 oz. wheat beer

3 dashes orange bitters

Add all ingredients except bitters to a pint glass. Add ice and shake. Strain the ingredients into a chilled cocktail glass, then top with orange bitters.

SERVING SUGGESTION:
Garnish with a lemon rind.

HORNY SICILIAN

MATTERHORN SKI BAR • NEWRY, MAINE

2 parts Hornitos Tequila

1 part Salerno Blood Orange Liquor from Sicily

1 lime wedge, juiced

Sour mix

Dash orange juice

EASIEST

Shake all ingredients together. In a salt-rimmed, 16 oz. glass, pour in cocktail.

POWDERHORN MOUNTAIN RESORT

THE MAD MIKE FIZZ

SUNSET GRILLE AND BAR • MESA, COLORADO

2 oz. Peachstreet Distillery Dark Rum

6 oz. Peachstreet Distillery Ginger Beer

2 lime slices, juiced

EASIEST

In a pint glass full of ice, add all ingredients together.

JAY PEAK RESORT

SNOWSHOE BLACK AND TAN

SNOWSHOE LODGE AND PUB • MONTGOMERY CENTER, VERMONT

Harpoon UFO

Guinness beer

EASIEST

In a 22 oz. Guinness glass, pour in Harpoon UFO until ⅔ full. Using a spoon to keep the liquids separate, pour in Guinness until glass is full.

WHISKEY GINGER COCKTAIL

10TH MOUNTAIN WHISKEY & SPIRIT CO. • VAIL, COLORADO

2 oz. 10th Mountain Rye Whiskey

1 Tbsp. honey

Ginger beer

Lemon slice

 EASIEST

Fill rocks glass with ice. Add whiskey, honey and top with ginger beer.

SERVING SUGGESTION:
Garnish cocktail with a lemon slice.

'DRINK TO GLORY' APRÈS SHOT

10TH MOUNTAIN WHISKEY & SPIRIT CO. • VAIL, COLORADO

1 ½ oz. 10th Mountain Rye Whiskey

½ oz. maple syrup

Pinch of cinnamon

 EASIEST

Add ingredients to a shaker full of ice. Shake well and strain into a shot glass.

SERVING SUGGESTION:
Tips up, bottoms up.

COLORADO MOON COCKTAIL

10TH MOUNTAIN WHISKEY & SPIRIT CO. • VAIL, COLORADO

1 ½ oz. Colorado Clear, Mountain Moonshine

2 oz. pineapple juice

½ oz. grenadine

½ oz. lemon-lime soda

Lime juice, freshly squeezed

1 cherry

 EASIEST

Mix together first 4 ingredients in a glass of your choice. Add freshly squeezed lime juice.

SERVING SUGGESTION:
Garnish with a cherry on top.

RUBY DREAM

FORMERLY OF SCANLON'S • BEND, OREGON

2 oz. Absolut Ruby Vodka

½ ruby grapefruit, juiced

1 lime wedge, muddled

Simple syrup to taste

SERVING SUGGESTION:
Garnish with a lime wheel.

 EASIEST

In a martini shaker, muddle lime wedge. Fill with ice. Add vodka, grapefruit juice and simple syrup. Shake until cold and serve.

HENDRICKS McTWIST

JOHN HARVARD'S BREW HOUSE • ELLICOTTVILLE, NEW YORK

1 oz. Hendricks Gin

1 oz. St. Germain

5 blueberries, fresh and plump

2 lemon slices

½ oz. simple syrup

3 oz. Champagne

Muddle fruit with liquor and simple syrup. Pour into a shaker and add ice. Shake well and pour into a small drink glass with ice. Cocktail creator Nicole Alter finishes this cocktail by topping it with Champagne.

SERVING SUGGESTION:
Garnish with blueberries and a lemon wedge.

HIGH FASHION

PLUMPJACK CAFÉ • OLYMPIC VALLEY, CALIFORNIA

1 ½ oz. Evan Williams Single Barrel Bourbon

½ oz. Lillet

½ oz. Amaro Montenegro

3 dashes Fee Brothers orange bitters

Splash Laphroaig Scotch

In a mixing glass, add first four ingredients. Add ice, shake, then strain into a martini glass rinsed with the scotch.

SERVING SUGGESTION:
Garnish with an orange twist.

RX RENEWAL

SNOWMASS KITCHEN AT THE WESTIN SNOWMASS RESORT • SNOWMASS, COLORADO

1 ½ oz. Bacardi

3 - 4 sage leaves, torn

½ tsp. smoked paprika

½ oz. lemon juice

½ oz. maple syrup

¼ tsp. star anise, crushed

Shake ingredients over ice and pour into ice-filled rocks glass.

SERVING SUGGESTION:
Top with a small sage leaf.

FIRESIDE MANHATTAN

BEANO'S CABIN • AVON, COLORADO

2 oz. Leopold Bros Maryland-Style
Rye Whiskey

1 oz. house-smoked sweet vermouth
(Carpano Antica Formula)

¼ oz. house-made vanilla bitters

EASIEST

Pour all into a mixing glass with ice cubes and stir well. Strain the drink into a cocktail glass.

SERVING SUGGESTION:
Garnish with two skewered Luxardo maraschino cherries.

MR. FIGGY

CROP BISTRO AND BREWERY • STOWE, VERMONT

2 oz. fig-infused bourbon

½ oz. sweet vermouth

2 dashes maple bitters

Candied bacon

EASIEST

Mix together all ingredients and serve up.

SERVING SUGGESTION:
Garnish with a piece of
candied bacon.

LARKSPUR RESTAURANT'S VAIL ICED TEA

VAIL MOUNTAIN COFFEE AND TEA COMPANY • VAIL, COLORADO

The V.I.T. (Vail Iced Tea) is one of the après ski specialty cocktails by Larkspur Restaurant. Affectionately referred to as the 'John Daly' for its close resemblance to a non-alcoholic Arnold Palmer (which combines equal parts iced tea and lemonade), this cocktail has been offered on the Après Ski menu for over 10 years.

2 oz. Vail Mountain Tea Company's Mango Ceylon Tea-Infused Vodka

4 oz. lemonade, fresh squeezed

MORE DIFFICULT

Pour Mango Ceylon Tea-Infused Vodka over ice cubes in a collins glass; add 4 oz. freshly-squeezed lemonade.

MANGO CEYLON TEA-INFUSED VODKA

½ cup loose Vail Mountain Tea Company's Mango Ceylon Tea

1 liter vodka of your choice

Fill a sealable glass container with vodka and tea. Steep up to 8 hours. After infusion is complete, strain through a fine sieve into a clean bottle. Store at room temperature.

SERVING SUGGESTION:
Garnish with a thinly sliced lemon wheel.

THE GUT SHOT

GRADY'S BAR • SILVERTON, COLORADO

½ glass Pabst Blue Ribbon

½ glass Red Bull

1 ½ oz. Jagermeister

EASIEST

Fill half a Solo Cup or pint glass with Pabst Blue Ribbon. Top with Red Bull. Pour the Jagermeister into a shot glass. Make a toast and drop the shot into the glass.

SNOWMASS SLING

ELK CAMP • SNOWMASS, COLORADO

1 ½ oz. Leopold Bros Gin

1 oz. fresh lemon juice

½ oz. cherry syrup

½ oz. grenadine

½ oz. Leopold Bros Alpine Herbal liqueur

2 oz. pineapple juice

½ oz. simple syrup

EASIEST

Shake together all ingredients.

SERVING SUGGESTION:
Serve over ice in a Collins glass.

S'MORETINI

OKEMO MOUNTAIN RESORT • CHEF SCOT EMERSON • LUDLOW, VERMONT

3 oz. marshmallow vodka

1 oz. Choco Lat

2 oz. Hershey's Chocolate Syrup

4 graham crackers

MORE DIFFICULT

Chill a martini glass. Crush graham crackers and place on a plate. On another plate, pour chocolate syrup. Dip the chilled glass into the chocolate syrup, covering the rim. Then, dip the glass into the graham crackers, covering the rim.

Fill a martini shaker with ice and pour in liquor. Shake and strain into the prepared martini glass.

WHITE CHOCOLATE WHITE RUSSIAN

ELK CAMP • SNOWMASS, COLORADO

1 oz. Cap Rock Vodka

1 oz. white crème de cacao

4 oz. half and half

EASIEST

Shake all ingredients together. Serve over ice.

SUN VALLEY RESORT

HOT TODDY

PIONEER SALOON • KETCHUM, IDAHO

1 cup very hot water

2 oz. Jack Daniels Tennessee Honey

1 tsp. Sugar in the Raw

Lemon wedge

Mix the first three ingredients and pour into a desired glass or mug.

SERVING SUGGESTION:
Bartender Dillon Witmer recommends serving this cocktail with a lemon wedge.

VAIL MOUNTAIN

GLUEHWEIN

SONNENALP RESORT • CHEF FLORIAN SCHWARZ • VAIL, COLORADO

1 ½ liters red wine

1 whole cinnamon

3 whole cloves

½ orange

1 lemon

2 whole allspice

1 star anise

Sugar to taste

MORE DIFFICULT

Add all ingredients in one pot and let it sit overnight. Boil and strain the spices. Add sugar to taste.

SERVING SUGGESTION:
Enjoy Lindsey Vonn's favorite après skiing cocktail warmed.

BASIN CONNECTION COCOA 2.0

CINNABAR LOUNGE • HUNTSVILLE, UTAH

1 ½ oz. Smirnoff Whipped Cream Vodka

½ oz. Crème de Cocoa

½ oz. Bailey's Cinnamon Vanilla

3 oz. hot cocoa (it must be piping hot as the liquor will cool the drink down)

Whipped cream, to taste

Shaved chocolate, to taste

1 cinnamon stick

MORE DIFFICULT

Combine first four ingredients in an Irish coffee mug, then top with whipped cream followed by the shaved chocolate.

SERVING SUGGESTION:
Garnish with a cinnamon stick.

BRIDGER BOWL SKI AREA

LOCO KOKOA

JIMMY B'S AT BRIDGER BOWL • BOZEMAN, MONTANA

1 oz. Jameson Irish Whiskey

1 oz. Bailey's Irish Cream

1 oz. Frangelico Liquor

4 oz. Hot Chocolate

Whipped Cream

EASIEST

Mix together first three ingredients. Add liquors to a mug of steaming hot chocolate.

SERVING SUGGESTION:
Top this comforting drink with whipped cream.

HOT BUTTERED RUM

BIERSTUBE • RED LODGE, MONTANA

2 heaping spoonfuls batter

2 oz. rum, your preference (Meyer's or Whaler's Dark Rum or spiced rum)

Hot water

When ready to enjoy a single serving, preheat a glass with hot water. Toss out the water and mix together batter and rum until it dissolves a little. Top the drink with *very* hot water. Stir until batter dissolves completely.

SERVING SUGGESTION:
Top the drink with whipped cream and cinnamon stick.

BATTER

½ cup unsalted butter

½ cup brown sugar

½ cup powdered sugar

2 Tbsp. honey

1 Tbsp. pumpkin spice

1 pint vanilla ice cream

Cinnamon stick, for garnish

Whipped cream, for garnish

Melt butter over medium-low heat. Slowly whisk in sugars until an even, almost paste-like consistency. Whisk in pumpkin spice and honey followed by the ice cream. When all the ice cream melts and the batter becomes very smooth and creamy, place in the freezer covered and let it set overnight.

HOT APPLE PIE

THE TERRACE AT HIGH CAMP • SQUAW VALLEY, CALIFORNIA

8 oz. hot apple cider

1 ½ oz. Tuaca

Combine ingredients.

SERVING SUGGESTION:
Top with whipped cream.

EXTERMINATOR COCKTAIL

SNORTING ELK CELLAR • CRYSTAL MOUNTAIN, WASHINGTON

This cocktail's namesake is the "Exterminator," a challenging double black diamond run that leads brave souls directly to the "Elk's" (as it's known on the mountain) backdoor. This difficult run with continuous pitch takes a skier +2000 vertical feet down the mountain to the base. The Exterminator cocktail, with a coffee base, surely provides a pick-me-up or nerve stabilizer to those bar patrons looking to warm up after a cold day on the slopes.

½ shot Bailey's Irish Cream

½ shot Kahlua

½ shot white rum

Fresh coffee, hot

Whipped cream

Mix together the liquors, then add hot, fresh coffee.

SERVING SUGGESTION:
Bartender John Rimelspach suggests topping the libation with whipped cream.

EL SABOR COFFEE

VAIL MOUNTAIN COFFEE AND TEA COMPANY & EL SABOR • VAIL, COLORADO

1 ½ oz. Herradura Anejo Tequila

½ oz. Tia Maria Vail Mountain Coffee

2 oz. heavy whipping cream

Mix together first two ingredients in a serving glass. In a separate shaker, add whipping cream and shake until frothy. Top coffee drink with whipped cream and dust with nutmeg.

SERVING SUGGESTION:
Adorn this cocktail with a cinnamon stick.

GARFINKEL'S COFFEE

VAIL MOUNTAIN COFFEE AND TEA COMPANY & GARFINKEL'S • VAIL, COLORADO

½ oz. butterscotch schnapps

½ oz. peppermint schnapps

½ oz. Saint Brendan's Irish Cream Liqueur

½ oz. Kahlua Coffee Liqueur

6 - 8 oz. Vail Mountain Coffee

Whipped cream

In a 10-oz. coffee mug, mix together liquors and hot coffee. Top with whipped cream.

SERVING SUGGESTION:
Enjoy after a cold day on the mountain!

BUENA VISTA IRISH COFFEE

MOUNTAIN STANDARD • VAIL, COLORADO

2 oz. Irish Whiskey

Vail Mountain Coffee (your choice), very hot

Whipped cream

Prepare one of your favorite coffees from Vail Mountain Coffee and Tea Company. Mix together first two ingredients in a glass mug.

SERVING SUGGESTION:
Top cocktail with whipped cream.

SKI TIP COFFEE

SKI TIP • KEYSTONE, COLORADO

¾ oz. Bailey's Irish Cream

½ oz. Grand Marnier

¼ oz. Dark Crème de Cocoa

Hot coffee

EASIEST

In a glass or mug of your choice, mix together first three ingredients, then top with very hot coffee.

SERVING SUGGESTION:
Finish the spiked coffee with whipped cream.

THE STANDARD COFFEE

MOUNTAIN STANDARD • DONOVAN SORNIG • VAIL, COLORADO

2 oz. Leopold Bros American Whiskey

Vail Mountain Coffee (your choice), very hot

Hand-whipped Malted Stout Cream

EASIEST

Prepare one of your favorite coffees from Vail Mountain Coffee and Tea Company. Mix together first two ingredients in a glass mug.

To make the hand-whipped malted stout cream, reduce stout in a saucepan. Cool and add malt extract. Fold this into cream.

SERVING SUGGESTION:
Top cocktail with stout cream.

Photography Credits

Michel Tallichet

Doug Marshall, El Photo Grande

Catrine Turillon

Ali Kaukas

Scott D W Smith, Imagesmith Photo

Craig Angevine, Yeahbudphotography.com

Jeremy Swanson, Jeremy Swanson Photo

Jackie Cooper, Jackie Cooper Photo

Matt Palmer / Squaw Valley

Josh Morton

Chad Chisholm, Custom Creations Photography

Matt Morgan

Sergio Howland

Russell Hurlburt, Russell Hurlburt Photography

Studio 404, Studio404photography.com

Lauren Turner

Court Leve Photography

Justin Peterson

Jen Holdeman

Fairweather Creative and Photography

Sandy Macys Photography

Winter Park Resort

Adam Brown

Christopher D Thompson Photography

Zach Mahone, Zach Mahone Photography

Billy Doran, Billy Doran Photographics

Kimberly Gavin, Kimberly Gavin Photography

Sharon Brezina, Brezina Design

Professional Acknowledgements

While my learning curve for my first cookbook (*Ski Town Soups*) assisted the ease of *Ski Town Après Ski*, I could not have completed this mouth-watering project without the help of others. Like the famous saying goes, "it takes a village." In this case, it took over 60 Ski villages to help the completion of this project. Thank you to the hotels: general managers and PR directors. Thank you to the ski resorts: marketing managers, PR directors and food and beverage directors. And, a generous thank you to the restaurants: general managers, executive and sous chefs and bartenders and mixologists. I have been fortunate enough to personally sample your cuisine and visit your luxurious restaurants; I feel blessed by the relationships that I've made with the pioneers of ski town cuisine.

Thank you, Franny Gustafson, for using your proofreading and copy-editing skills, which you honed at HarperCollins and Pearson. Your precise, eagle eye sharpened a manuscript, of which I am very proud. I am also truly appreciative for all the effort and care from Lindsey Vonn, Jenny Murphy, and Sue Dorf in creating a wonderful foreword compilation for this cookbook.

Finally, and most importantly, I appreciate and am indebted to you: Jay Monroe, James Monroe Design. Your creativity and artistry in this book, as well as *Ski Town Soups*, has been unparalleled and unmatched. It has been a delight to work with you, and I feel very accomplished with the end product we produced. I have thoroughly enjoyed trusting you with this very significant project. The design, layout, attention to detail along with your supportive and relaxed personality eased the creation process. Thank you very much and I hope for continued success with other projects!

Personal Dedications

I thank my extended family members for supporting this project with encouragements and suggestions. You are wonderful promoters of my craft, and for that I am grateful.

My most important dedication is to Ross, my steadfast husband, patient business partner, true confidante, ultimate best friend and loving beacon of support, encouragement and understanding. Like through the first project, you have endured the highs and lows of the creative process—being a tolerant sounding board, supportive financial outlet and a calm, cool and collected motivator. I am astounded and thrilled that *Ski Town Après Ski* came together so swiftly and effortlessly; for that I owe my entire gratitude to you. Thank you for making me want to create the best project I can. I strive to make you proud! Thank you again for fitting *Ski Town Après Ski* into your *über*-demanding professional life and letting it trickle over to our personal life.

Finally, to my sons who thoughtfully ask me, if not daily, than weekly, "how is Après going, Mom?" My sons grasp my previous cookbook, *Ski Town Soups*, and exclaim about their favorite recipes, or reminisce about our travels, or proclaim what a great cook I am. So, to my little masters, I am humbled by your praise and hope that you always consider me "famous." I am thrilled that I can make you proud, as my most important love in life is family. Because of you, I am stronger and more inspired each day. I promise to always be there for you after a day on the mountain!

INDEX

Chefs

Bartenders/Mixologists

About the Author

Jennie Iverson is the best-selling author of *Ski Town Soups, Ski Town Apres Ski* and *Ski Town Brunch*. Jennie, who lives in Vail, Colorado, is also a wife and a mother of 3 fast-growing boys with healthy, enormous appetites. After savoring days on the mountain, Jennie and her family enjoy "special drinks" and snacks around the fire, sharing stories about the day's events.

Jennie considers herself a gourmet in the kitchen, but more evidently a gourmand—enjoying restaurants, bistros and any dining establishment where she can sit down to others' creations. She also thoroughly enjoys traveling to other ski towns, as she relishes locals who take advantage of the out-of-doors and surrounding mountains. To sample some of the best soups for *Ski Town Soups,* appetizers and drinks for *Ski Town Apres Ski*, and beginning of the day dishes for *Ski Town Brunch,* Jennie has traveled to Sun Valley, Jackson Hole, Mt Bachelor, Mt. Hood, Whitefish Mountain, Big Sky, Moonlight Basin, Heavenly, Northstar, Park City, Vail, Beaver Creek, Breckenridge, Copper Mountain, Aspen Highlands, Aspen Mountain, Snowmass, Buttermilk, Bretton Woods, Canyons, Deer Valley, Keystone, Killington, Mad River Glen, Sugarbush, Okemo, Smugglers' Notch, Steamboat, Stowe, Stratton and Whiteface. What has grown from these travel experiences has been a perfectly balanced recipe for life: a ski town, a comfortable restaurant and a yummy food dish to share with the family. Reaffirming that one should raise a glass in a toast, more often.

Professionally and following the launch of these cookbooks, Jennie has relished in many extraordinary culinary opportunities: guest judging the Lake Tahoe soup-cooking competition, launching the inaugural Park City Soup Crawl, guest appearances at The Cottage at Mirror Lake and Omni Mount Washington Resort, covering the Stowe Wine & Food Classic, authoring monthly articles for the *Vail Daily*, blogging about Aspen's SoupSkol competition and following many renowned food events, such as Feast!Vail, Beaver Creek Food & Wine Festival, Taste of Vail, Cochon555, Denver Burger Battle, Blues, Brews and BBQ and Gourmet on Gore.

Jennie Iverson has quickly become a foremost expert on ski town cuisine.